Travel Guide To Venice 2023

Venice 2023: An Up-to-Date Travel Guide to the City's Best"

Scott O. Cortes

Table of Contents

Final Thoughts and Recommendations
Fond Farewell to Venice

INTRODUCTION

Thank you for visiting "Travel Guide to Venice 2023: An Up-To-Date Travel Guide to the City's Best." As the "Queen of the Adriatic," Venice is a captivating city known for its alluring canals, magnificent architecture, and extensive history.

This book is intended to improve your experience and give you the most recent information and insider ideas for seeing Venice in 2023, whether you're a first-time visitor or an experienced traveller.

This travel book intends to be your all-encompassing travel companion, providing a wealth of information about Venice's big attractions, hidden jewels, cultural nuances, and useful tips. We can help you with everything from travel planning to navigating the maze-like streets of the city. We want to ensure that every moment you spend in Venice is filled with wonder and astonishment. This way, you can make the most of your stay here.

Practical Information: You'll find helpful advice in this guide to help you get ready for your adventure in Venice. To ensure a smooth and pleasurable trip, we'll go over issues including the best time to visit, how to get to Venice, money-saving advice, visa requirements, and other pertinent information. During your stay, we want you to feel prepared and have the information you need to make wise decisions.

So, this travel book will be your dependable travel companion whether you're entranced by the romance of the gondolas, anxious to explore the famed St. Mark's Square, or fascinated by the city's hidden gems. Let us reveal the secrets and beauties that await you in 2023 as we take you on a voyage through Venice's winding canals, magnificent bridges, and alluring culture. The journey has begun!

Welcome to Venice

Welcome to Venice, a unique city. Venice is a genuine masterpiece of art, architecture, and history, located in the picturesque Venetian Lagoon in northeastern Italy. You will be carried away to a world of timeless beauty and alluring charm as soon as you set foot on its historic cobblestone streets and explore its intricate network of canals.

Venice has always captivated the hearts of tourists from all over the world with its romantic gondolas sailing along the waterways and its towering palaces rising from the depths. As the "City of Canals," Venice connects her 118 islands with a complex network of waterways, lending an ethereal quality to the city's already beautiful atmosphere.

In Venice, there is a fresh sight to admire around each corner. Visitors are in awe of the city's architectural wonders, which range from the renowned St. Mark's Square, which is dominated by the splendour of St. Mark's Basilica and the elaborate Doge's Palace, to the charming Rialto Bridge over the busy Grand Canal. Explore secret treasures tucked away in tiny alleyways, chance upon gorgeous piazzas brimming with bustling cafes, or meander through tranquil districts, each with its unique flavour.

Venice is another city rich in culture and history. Explore the city's world-class museums with works by renowned artists, delve into its colourful customs that have defined its identity, and learn about its illustrious past as a maritime power. Enjoy delicious cicchetti (little snacks), superb wines, and the flavours of authentic Venetian cuisine while taking in the wonderful ambiance that permeates every meal.

Venice guarantees a memorable experience, whether you're drawn to the city for its art, history, and romance, or just to get lost in its maze-like alleyways. Allow yourself to be enthralled by the essence of Venice, where the symbiotic interaction of land and water creates an environment that is both magical and steeped in history.

Let this travel book serve as your compass as you set out on your voyage through the Venetian canals. It offers insights, suggestions, and useful guidance to help you make the most of your time in Venice. In 2023, get ready to be enchanted as you discover this extraordinary city's attractions. Greetings from Venice, the crowning glory of Italy's Adriatic coast.

GETTING TO KNOW VENICE

As you explore this enchanted city's special qualities, history, and culture, getting to know Venice is an exhilarating task. Here are some crucial details to help you get to know Venice:

- Geographically speaking, Venice is a series of islands in a lagoon in northeastern Italy. It is constructed on 118 little islands connected by canals, and a causeway connects it to the mainland.

- Venice is well-known for its complex canal system, which is the main mode of transportation within the city. Venice's major canal, the Grand Canal, is flanked by spectacular palaces and structures.

- **Architecture**: Venice has a rich history of different architectural styles. The structures in the city are examples of a synthesis of influences over the ages, ranging from Byzantine and Gothic to Renaissance and Baroque styles. The Doge's Palace and St. Mark's Basilica are well-known examples of Venetian design.

- **Venetian Gothic**: Venice is well-known for its distinctive architectural design, ornate detailing, pointed arches, and ornamental embellishments. To appreciate its unique design, visit structures like the Ca' d'Oro and the Scuola Grande di San Marco.

- **Venetian Lagoon:** The city's environs, the Venetian Lagoon, are a UNESCO World Heritage site. With a variety of plants and animals, including marshlands, islands, and sandbanks, it is a delicate ecology. The lagoon is essential to the preservation and history of Venice.

- **Historical Importance:** During the Middle Ages and the Renaissance, Venice was a significant centre of trade, art, and culture. It was also once a strong maritime republic. With the Byzantine Empire, the Ottoman Empire, and other European superpowers like France and Austria, it has a shared history.

- **Carnival of Venice**: Before the start of Lent, this acclaimed annual festival is known around the world. It draws tourists from all over the world due to its spectacular masks, costumes, and festivities.

- Featuring shellfish, risotto, polenta, and classic dishes like sarde in saor and baccalà mantecato, Venetian cuisine is a gourmet treat. Don't pass up the chance to indulge in cicchetti, little nibbles best eaten with a glass of wine and local delicacies.

- **Art and Culture:** Throughout history, Venice has been a hub of outstanding artistic and cultural endeavours. Reputable art museums with a diverse collection of works, such as the Peggy Guggenheim Collection and Gallerie dell'Accademia, may be found there.

- **Local customs:** The culture of the people of Venice is extensive, and it includes customs like gondola rowing, glassblowing in Murano, producing lace in Burano, and the Festa del

Redentore, a stunning annual event with a fireworks display.

Investigating these facets will enhance your knowledge of and admiration for Venice, enabling you to embrace its distinctive personality and submerge yourself in the city's alluring atmosphere. Enjoy learning about Venice as you travel there!

A Brief History of Venice

The history of Venice is a remarkable story of tenacity, cunning, and magnificence. Venetian exiles fleeing barbarian assaults on the Italian mainland founded the city-state in the fifth century AD.

From a group of marshy islands, Venice developed into a potent maritime republic that controlled trade in the Mediterranean for centuries.

- **The Early Years:** With its network of islands and waterways, the Venetian lagoon offered a natural defence and enabled the earliest residents to create a self-governing community. Venice had developed into a city-state with a distinct political structure by the ninth century. The head of the government during Venice's heyday was an elected figure known as the Doge.

- Venice's strategic location at the meeting point of East and West contributed to its growth as a naval power and its subsequent commercial empire. Commercial ties were established with Byzantium, the Islamic world, and the Crusader powers by the city's merchant ships, which dominated trade routes.

The Renaissance was fueled by the enormous wealth collected by Venetian traders who also brought exotic commodities and ideas to Europe.

- **The Republic of Venice:** Under the control of an aristocratic elite, Venice thrived as a republic. Due to its riches, great palaces, grand churches, and famous landmarks were built. Three iconic representations of Venice's wealth and artistic prowess are St. Mark's Basilica, the Doge's Palace, and the Rialto Bridge.

- **Conflict and Decline:** Over the years, Venice's authority and influence experienced difficulties. Venetian resources were taxed by conflict with competing city-states like Genoa and territory issues. The city's influence was weakened by the discovery of alternative trade routes that did not use the Mediterranean. Additionally, the population suffered greatly from the Black Death outbreak in the 14th century.

- **The Decline of the Republic:** By the late 18th century, Napoleon Bonaparte had taken over the authority of the Republic of Venice, which was thereafter ruled by Austria. The heyday of the city as an autonomous republic was over. Venice joined the Kingdom of Italy in 1866.

- **Venice Today:** Today's Venice is a thriving cultural centre and UNESCO World Heritage site. The city continues to draw tourists from all over the world with the help of its architectural wonders, art collections, and yearly events like the Venice Biennale.

Venice continues to be a city of outstanding beauty and cultural significance despite difficulties brought on by increasing sea levels and excessive tourists.

The intricate palaces, winding lanes, and romantic ambiance of Venice in 2023 will bring its illustrious past to life as you wander the city. Knowing Venice's past helps you appreciate both its ongoing legacy and the extraordinary experience you are about to take.

Geography and Layout of the City

The extraordinary city of Venice is located in the Venetian Lagoon, a sizable shallow bay on Italy's northeastern coast. Its unique layout and geographic location both add to its alluring beauty and set it apart from other cities in the world.

- **The Venetian Lagoon**: Venice comprises 118 tiny islands connected by a system of canals, spaced apart by constricting waterways, and connected by more than 400 bridges. A 50-kilometre-long lagoon separates the city from the open sea naturally. It spans the Adriatic Sea.

- The principal islands of Venice are divided into six sestieri districts or districts. Each sestiere has a distinct personality and draws:

- **San Marco:** The Doge's Palace, St. Mark's Square (Piazza San Marco), and various stores, cafes, and historical sites are all found in this sestiere in the centre of Venice.

- With its residential areas, charming canals, and Jewish Ghetto, Cannaregio, the largest and most populous sestiere in Venice, provides a window into everyday life in the region.

- **The Accademia Gallery**, the Peggy Guggenheim Collection, and the lovely promenade along the Zattere shoreline are all located in the neighbourhood of Dorsoduro, which is renowned for its artistic and cultural treasures.

- Castello, the largest sestiere geographically, is home to the historic Arsenale shipyards, the bustling Via Garibaldi, and the serene Giardini public gardens.

- **Santa Croce**: This town includes a combination of residential areas and ancient buildings, such as the Church of San Simeon Grande and the Ca' Pesaro art museum. Santa Croce is located close to the bus and train stations.

- **San Polo:** This neighbourhood includes the bustling Rialto Market, the second-largest square in the city, the lively Campo San Polo, and the Rialto Bridge.

- **Waterways & Canals**: The canals are Venice's transit hub, taking the place of the city's streets. The Grand Canal, the city's major waterway, meanders through the centre of Venice and is flanked on both sides by spectacular palaces and ancient structures. The Cannaregio Canal, the Giudecca Canal, as well as the lesser Rio di San Barnaba and Rio di San Polo, are further noteworthy canals.

- **Bridges**: Venetian islands are connected by an astounding number of bridges that cross over canals. The Rialto Bridge, a stunning stone arch bridge that has stood as a representation of Venice for centuries, is the most well-known. The Accademia Bridge, the Scalzi Bridge, and the Bridge of Sighs are a few further noteworthy bridges.

Navigating Venice's distinctive transit system, discovering its varied neighbourhoods, and appreciating the beauty of its canals and bridges all need an understanding of the city's topography and layout. Allow Venice's beautiful geography to lead you through an adventure that will live long in the memory as you navigate the maze-like streets and cruise along the waterways.

Venetian Culture and Traditions

Venice is a destination rich in culture and customs in addition to being a city of canals and stunning architecture. Venice's distinctive way of life, which is reflected in its art, music, cuisine, and social norms, is formed by its unique history and physical location. Discover the following aspects of Venetian heritage and culture:

- **Carnival:** The Carnival, a centuries-old celebration that takes place in the weeks preceding Lent, is one of Venice's most well-known customs. The streets come alive with vibrant masks, elaborate costumes, and exuberant celebrations during Carnival.

  The "Flight of the Angel," in which a predetermined performer descends from St. Mark's Campanile to the centre of St.

Mark's Square, is the biggest event.

- **Gondolas & Gondoliers**: The gondola is a well-known emblem of Venice and is a typical Venetian rowing boat. The expert boatmen known as gondoliers, who operate these exquisite boats, are fundamental to Venetian culture.

  Gondoliers offer romantic rides down the canals, complete with serenades and historical narratives, and are easily identifiable by their striped shirts and straw hats.

- **Making of Venetian Masks**: Venice is well-known for its elaborate masks, which have a long tradition rooted in the city's Carnival celebrations. The craft of creating Venetian masks has existed since the 13th century.

Originally, individuals from all walks of life donned these masks, which were frequently embellished with feathers, gems, and bright colours, to hide their identities and social standing during Carnival. Venetian masks are still worn at festivals and masquerade balls today and are a common gift.

- **Venetian Glass:** With a history of more than a thousand years, Venice is recognized for its excellent glassmaking technique. The hub of this historic craft is the island of Murano, which is close to Venice.

Glassblowers in Venice are renowned for their proficiency in many techniques, including blowing, sculpting, and etching glass to produce complicated and exquisite items, such as chandeliers, vases, and jewellery.

- The delicious flavour fusion of Venetian food is a result of its nautical heritage and closeness to the water. In meals like baccalà mantecato (creamed cod), risotto al nero di seppia (squid ink risotto), and sarde in saor (marinated sardines), fresh seafood is the star.

In Venice's bacari (wine bars), Cicchetti, little savoury snacks frequently served with a glass of wine, are very well-liked.

- **Regata Storica:** Honouring Venice's long-standing association with rowing, Regata Storica is a classic Venetian rowing competition held on the Grand Canal. In a variety of races, gondoliers dressed historically compete, while onlookers line the canal banks to support their favourite teams.

- **Venetian dialect:** Some inhabitants still use the Venetian dialect, a distinctive variation of the Italian language. Even though Italian is widely spoken and understood, the Venetian dialect's distinctive rhythm and lexicon give the city of Venice a more real feel.

A fuller comprehension of the city's identity and the lives of its citizens can be gained by investigating Venetian culture and traditions. These cultural components, which range from the brilliant hues of Carnival to the deft artistry of Venetian glass, add to the magical ambiance that makes Venice exceptional.

PLANNING YOUR TRIP

To make the most of your time in this intriguing city, meticulous planning and preparation are essential while travelling to Venice. When organising your trip to Venice in 2023, bear the following important considerations in mind:

- **Best Time to Visit**: Since Venice sees a lot of tourists, it's crucial to pick the best time to go. The summer months (June to August), when crowds are at their heaviest, are the busiest in the city. For better weather and fewer visitors, consider travelling in the shoulder seasons of spring (April to May) or autumn (September to October).

  Although the winter months of November to February offer a more tranquil atmosphere, be prepared for cooler weather and sporadic floods (acqua alta).

- Depending on your interests and the things you want to do, decide how long you want to spend in Venice. Even while it is possible to see the city's top attractions in a couple of days, staying for at least three to four days enables a more leisurely and immersive experience.

  To add variation to your itinerary, think about taking day trips to adjacent islands like Murano, Burano, or Torcello.

- **Accommodations:** There are many different types of lodging available in Venice to accommodate a variety of interests and price ranges. There is accommodation for every tourist, from opulent hotels with canal views to a warm bed and breakfasts nestled away in quiet areas. The best way to see the key landmarks is to stay in the city's core, close to places like St. Mark's Square or the Rialto Bridge. As an alternative, think about staying in less populated locations to feel more at home.

- Venice is easily accessible from many major Italian and European cities. Flying into Marco Polo Airport, which is on the mainland, is the most popular route to get to the city.

To get to the city centre from the airport, you can take a bus, taxi, or boat transfer (vaporetto or water taxi). Arriving by train is an additional choice, as the Grand Canal is near the Santa Lucia train station in Venice.

- Venice is a pedestrian-friendly city, and within its historic district, walking is the main form of transit. Learn the layout of the city, carry a thorough map, or use navigation software to get around the bridges and tight streets.

  Vaporettos (water buses) offer transportation along the main canals and to the distant islands, making them a convenient mode of transportation. To enjoy unlimited rides throughout your visit, think about buying a travel pass.

- **Sightseeing & Attractions:** There are many sights to visit and landmarks to discover in Venice. Set St. Mark's Basilica, the Doge's Palace, the Rialto Bridge, and the Grand Canal as your top priorities. To save time and avoid lengthy lines at popular attractions, think about purchasing skip-the-line tickets in advance. Utilise guided tours to learn more about the history, culture, and art of Venice.

- When visiting Venice, be respectful of the regional traditions and customs. When visiting churches and other sacred buildings, dress modestly by covering your knees and shoulders. Be considerate to your neighbours and limit noise, especially in residential areas. Keep in mind that Venice is a lively city where residents spend their daily time in the streets and canals.

- **Budgeting:** Venice, especially in the busiest tourist regions, may be pricey. Consider the costs of lodging, meals, transportation, and attractions while creating your budget. Explore the neighbourhood markets for fresh food and snacks, and look for neighbourhood trattorias and osterias for inexpensive eating options. A Venice City Pass or Museum Pass can be worth buying if you want to access several sites at a price.

You can guarantee a smooth journey and a great experience in one of the world's most captivating cities by meticulously organising your vacation to Venice.

Best Time to Visit

The ideal time to visit Venice will depend on your choices and the experiences you hope to have while there. For guidance, consider the following descriptions of Venice's many seasons:

- The months of April and May are prime for visiting Venice. With temperatures ranging from 10°C to 20°C (50°F to 68°F), the climate is often warm and pleasant.

  The city begins to come to life as a result of the blooming flowers and vivid hues. The tourist season officially starts in the spring, but it is still less busy than in the summer. Remember that there may be sporadic downpours.

- **Summer (June to August):** In Venice, summer is the busiest travel period. The city experiences a sizable influx of tourists, and popular destinations can get busy. Temperatures range from 20°C to 30°C (68°F to 86°F) and are warm and muggy.

  Although there are more people throughout the summer, the longer daylight hours allow you to take advantage of the city's beauty well into the evening. If travelling during this period, think about making reservations for lodging and attractions.

- **Autumn (September to October):** The fall is a wonderful season to visit Venice. With temperatures ranging from 12°C to 22°C (54°F to 72°F), the weather is quite pleasant. You may take advantage of a more laid-back attitude while still experiencing good weather as the summer crowds start to thin out. Autumn is also a period for festivals and cultural events like the Festa del Redentore and the Venice International Film Festival.

- **Winter (November to February):** Venice is quieter and less congested throughout the winter, making it a great time for visitors looking for a more personal and genuine experience. With temperatures ranging from 0°C to 10°C (32°F to 50°F), the climate can be chilly.

  During this time, there may be sporadic flooding (acqua alta). However, the winter has its allure, particularly around the holidays when the city is festooned with lights and ornaments. It's a wonderful time to visit museums, unwind in inviting cafes, and take in the Venetian way of life.

The best times to visit Venice are frequently in the shoulder seasons of spring (April to May) and autumn (September to October), taking into account things like weather, crowds, and individual tastes.

These times offer a good mix of agreeable weather, reasonable people, and a lively environment. The best time to visit Venice depends on your interests and priorities, although each season has its allure.

Duration of Stay

The perfect length of time to spend in Venice depends on several things, including your interests, your time constraints, and what you hope to experience there.

While it is easy to see the main attractions in Venice in one or two days, spending more time there offers a more comprehensive and complete experience. You can use the following factors to determine how long you will stay:

- **Sightseeing**: St. Mark's Square, the Doge's Palace, the Rialto Bridge, as well as several churches and museums, are just a few of the many attractions available in Venice. Plan for a minimum of two to three full days if you wish to visit these important areas of interest and explore these well-known landmarks. You'll have enough time to enjoy the city's fascinating architecture and history.

- **Island hopping:** The city of Venice extends beyond its main island. Consider taking day trips to adjacent islands like Burano, which is well-known for its lace manufacturing and colourful homes, and Murano, which is renowned for its glassmaking heritage. Depending on how many islands you choose to see, adding these island trips to your plan can take an extra day or two.

- **Cultural Events:** Throughout the year, Venice plays host to several festivals and cultural events, including the Venice Biennale, Carnival, and the Historical Regatta. If you intend to attend any of these events, provide extra time so that you may fully take part in the fun and appreciate the distinctive experiences they have to offer.

- **Relaxation and exploration**: A slow pace is excellent for enjoying Venice. Give yourself enough time to roam around the camping (small alleys) and the campi (secret squares). Enjoy leisurely gondola rides along the canals, authentic Venetian fare at neighbourhood trattorias, and just take in the atmosphere of this magical city. A couple of extra days will enable a more unhurried and all-encompassing experience.

- Given the aforementioned considerations, a minimum of three to four full days would be advised for a comprehensive trip to Venice. This amount of time enables you to see the main sights, go to adjacent islands for a day, and enjoy some downtime and private exploration. Nevertheless, if you have more time, extending your stay to a week or more will allow you to learn more about the city's culture, traditions, and undiscovered jewels.

In the end, the length of your stay should reflect your preferences and interests to guarantee that you have an enjoyable and memorable time in Venice..

Budgeting and Expenses in Venice

Venice is renowned for its allure and beauty, but it's vital to take into account the price of travelling there. When making a travel budget for your trip to Venice, bear the following things in mind:

- **Accommodations:** Depending on the area, the type of lodging, and the time of year, the cost of lodging in Venice can vary significantly. Hotels with views of canals or close to popular sites are typically more expensive.

  To cut costs, think about staying in less convenient regions or looking into other lodging choices like bed and breakfasts or holiday rentals. It's a good idea to make reservations in advance, especially during busy tourist times.

- **Meals:** There are a variety of dining alternatives in Venice, from cheap eats to upscale establishments. Find neighbourhood trattorias and osterias that serve reasonably priced traditional fare to reduce your dining expenses. Try cicchetti (little tapas-style dishes) and browse the fresh food and snack aisles at your neighbourhood markets.

  Eat away from popular tourist destinations because the cost of food there is often greater. To help you manage spending, think about allocating a daily budget for food.

- Public transit and walking are the two main ways to get to Venice. The Vaporetto (water bus), a much-liked means of transportation, offers single tickets as well as multi-day travel permits.

If you intend to use the Vaporetto regularly while visiting, think about buying a trip card. Although more expensive, private water taxis provide a more upscale experience. If you intend to take a gondola ride, keep in mind that they can be expensive tourist activities, so account for this in your budget.

- **Sightseeing and Attractions:** There are many attractions in Venice, many of which charge admission. Make an agenda and look into the cost of the sites you want to see. To save time and avoid lengthy lines, skip-the-line tickets are available for some attractions, including St. Mark's Basilica.

  Look for combo passes or combination tickets that provide

discounted entry to several attractions.

- Venice is renowned for its distinctive souvenirs, such as Murano glass, Venetian masks, and handcrafted lace. Set a spending limit and pay attention to the authenticity and quality of the goods you buy. Look for affordable solutions at regional markets, like the Rialto Market, and think about promoting local craftsmen.

- It's crucial to account for extra costs like travel insurance, transportation to and from Venice, and any day trips or activities you intend to go on. A contingency budget should also be set aside for unforeseen costs or crises.

- In general, visiting Venice can be pricey, especially in popular tourist areas. However, you can control your costs and have a memorable event without going overboard if you plan, make a budget, and choose wisely. You may maximise your spending while discovering Venice's beauties by doing price comparisons, thinking about other possibilities, and asking around for ideas.

Visa Requirements and Travel Documents for Venice

Make sure you have the required travel documents in order before organising your vacation to Venice. Here is a list of the necessary travel documents and visa requirements you could need:

- **Visa Requirements:** Depending on your country, the reason for your trip, and how long you plan to stay, Venice may require a visa. If you are a non-citizen of the European Union (EU), you must familiarise yourself with the visa requirements for Italy or the Schengen Area because Venice is located in Italy.

  In general, EU residents do not need a visa to enter Italy, including Venice. The most recent visa rules should always be checked, though, as they are subject to change.

- You must determine if you need a Schengen visa if you are a citizen of a non-EU nation. It is possible to enter and move around the Schengen Area, which includes Italy, with a Schengen visa.

  The standard procedure for applying for a visa entails providing the necessary paperwork, including a current passport, evidence of travel insurance, information about where you'll be staying, proof of your ability to pay, and a completed application form. It is advised to submit your visa application well in advance of the trip you intend to take.

- **Passport**: For international travel to Venice, a current passport is required. Make sure your passport is valid for at least six months after the day you intend to depart. Examine your passport's expiration date and, if necessary, renew it. Making duplicates of your passport and keeping them in a different location is also a smart idea in case it is lost or stolen.

- **Travel insurance:** It is strongly advised to get travel insurance when visiting Venice or any other foreign location. Medical crises, trip cancellations or interruptions, lost or delayed luggage, and other unanticipated events are all covered by travel insurance.

Make sure your travel insurance provides sufficient coverage for your needs and covers the entire duration of your trip.

- Booking your flight tickets in advance is required if you intend to travel to Venice by air. To get the greatest bargains, compare prices offered by several airlines and think about making a reservation far in advance. Make sure the name on your passport and the one on the airline ticket match.

- **Proof of Accommodation:** Immigration officials may request proof of lodging for the duration of your stay when you enter Venice.

  If you're staying with friends or family, this could take the form of hotel bookings, a booking confirmation from a vacation rental, or an invitation letter from the host. Make sure you have the required paperwork on hand to show when you arrive.

It's crucial to keep in mind that visa requirements and guidelines for travel documents can vary, so it's advised to check with the relevant Italian or domestic embassy or consulate well in advance of your trip. For your particular scenario, they will offer the most recent and correct information on visa requirements and travel documentation.

NAVIGATING VENICE

Exploring Venice's distinctive network of canals, winding alleyways, and gorgeous bridges may be an exhilarating journey. Here are some pointers to help you successfully traverse the city:

- Study a map to become familiar with Venice's layout before going there. Look over a map of the area and make a note of the key bridges, canals, and landmarks. You'll have a sense of direction and be able to plan your routes thanks to this.

- **Utilise Landmarks and Signposts:** Venice is dotted with signposts that direct you to important landmarks, transportation hubs, and districts. Look for signs leading in the direction of well-known locations like St. Mark's Square or the Rialto

Bridge (Ponte di Rialto). Use recognizable sites like churches or palaces as guides as well to help you get about.

- **Follow the Arrows:** All across Venice, arrow signs painted on walls and pavement lead to important landmarks or busy locations. To find your way to the important areas of interest, follow these arrows.

- **Explore on Foot:** Walking is frequently the easiest method to get through Venice's confined streets and lanes (referred to as "calli"). Allowing yourself to become lost in the confusing streets can result in surprising discoveries and undiscovered treasures. Keep in mind that you'll be walking through numerous bridges and difficult terrain, so wear appropriate walking shoes.

- Consider the vaporetto, a type of water vehicle that is the main form of public transit in Venice. They run along the city's canals and link various areas of Venice and the nearby islands.

For unrestricted travel on the vaporetto throughout your visit, think about getting a pass or purchase single tickets as required. Stops for the vaporetto are properly marked, and schedules are available there or online.

- **Think about Private Water Taxis:** You can hire a water taxi if you want a more direct and private way of transportation. Although more expensive than vaporettos, water taxis provide convenience and a more individualised experience. They can be obtained through hotels or taxi companies, or they can be found at designated taxi stands.

- **Cross the Canals**: Venice is renowned for its stunning bridges that link the various neighbourhoods of the city. You will encounter a lot of bridges as you travel through the canals. Use them as landmarks when exploring the city and pay attention to the signs pointing in the direction of the closest bridge.

- **Accept the Vaporetto Traghetti**: At select spots, these gondola-like boats are used to cross the Grand Canal. They offer a quick and convenient route to cross the canal and are mainly used by residents. Join the locals who are taking the ferry across the sea by looking for the Traghetti signage.

- **Use GPS or Navigation Apps**: Use a GPS or navigation app on your smartphone if you're worried about getting lost. Even amid the convoluted alleyways of Venice, these applications can direct you and provide you turn-by-turn directions.

- Don't be afraid to seek assistance if you find yourself lost or in need of direction. Typically helpful and prepared to offer advice, the locals are kind. There are also numerous tourist information centres located throughout the city where you may get directions, maps, and pamphlets.

- Take your time, take in Venice's distinct atmosphere, and take pleasure in discovering this magnificent city.

Transportation Options

Venice provides a variety of transit choices to make getting around the city easier. The primary forms of transportation are as follows:

- **Walking**: Venice is a pedestrian-friendly city, so exploring it on foot is frequently the best option. The majority of the major sights are accessible on foot, and getting lost in the labyrinthine lanes can result in exciting discoveries.

- Water buses known as vaporettos travel across Venice's canals. They connect several areas of the city, including the islands of Murano, Burano, and Lido, and are a crucial form of public transit. Tickets for vaporettos can be purchased through authorised vendors, ticket booths, or ticket machines at vaporetto stops.

Vaporettos operate on a variety of lines. If you intend to use vaporettos frequently while visiting, think about buying a travel pass.

- Private boats known as "water taxis" provide a more upscale and efficient mode of transportation in Venice. They are more expensive than vaporettos but speedier and more adaptable. At designated taxi stands, passengers can call for a water taxi or make arrangements with hotels or taxi services. If you're short on time or want a more tailored experience, they provide a practical choice.

- **Traghetti**: At various spots, gondola-like boats called traghetti are used to cross the Grand Canal. These boats offer a quick and convenient way to cross the canal and are mainly used by locals.

Traghetti is a localised transportation option that can be used instead of the closest bridge.

- **Gondolas**: Although they are recognizable emblems of Venice, gondolas are more commonly employed for tourists than for actual transportation. Gondola rides are more expensive than other forms of transportation, but they can be a romantic and relaxing way to explore the city's canals. Near famous tourist destinations, gondolas can be found; the cost is frequently negotiable.

- Bicycles are permitted on the Lido island, which has wider streets and designated bike pathways, despite the fact that walking is the predominant form of transportation in Venice. Lido's sandy beaches and the island itself can be enjoyed by renting bicycles.

- **Water ferries**: These larger vessels go between Venice and adjacent locations including the train station, the airport, and other islands. These ferries make it easy to travel to nearby islands for the day or to get to Venice from the mainland. Online or at the ferry ports are the two places to buy tickets.

- **Taxis and private** vehicles are not permitted in Venice's historic district. However, the closest locations that are reachable by car are Piazzale Roma or Tronchetto, where taxis can drop you off. You can either continue on foot or switch to vaporettos or water taxis from there.

Consider your stay in Venice's length, the distance you need to travel, your spending limit, and the type of experience you want to have when selecting a mode of transportation. In the intriguing city of Venice, a mix of strolling, vaporettos, and sporadic rides on water taxis or gondolas can offer a well-rounded and pleasurable transit experience.

Getting in to and from the airport

When visiting Venice, getting to and from the airport is an important component of your trip. The following are the primary means of transportation you have to choose from to get to the city centre or your lodging:

Airport at Marco Polo (VCE):

- **Bus**: The "Fly Bus" operated by the ACTV bus company travels from Marco Polo Airport to Piazzale Roma, the entrance to the historic city of Venice. Buses run frequently throughout the day, taking around 20 minutes to complete the trip.

- **Water Bus (Alilaguna)**: Alilaguna water buses offer a beautiful way to go from the airport to Venice. From the airport, the Orange, Blue, and Red lines travel to a number of locations throughout Venice, including San Marco and Rialto. Depending on the route and destination, the trip lasts about an hour.

- **Water Taxi**: For a more opulent and direct ride to your destination in Venice, there are private water taxis accessible at the airport. Although they can be pricey, water taxis provide a handy and individualised service.

Airport of Treviso (TSF):

- **Shuttle Bus:** ATVO runs a shuttle bus service between the Piazzale Roma in Venice and the Treviso Airport. Buses leave often to match flight arrivals for the roughly 70-minute trip.

- **Train**: To get to Treviso Centrale train station from Treviso Airport, take a local bus or taxi. The Santa Lucia train station in Venice can be reached by taking a train from there. About 30 to 40 minutes are needed for the train ride.

- When you arrive in Venice, you have two options: either carry on to your lodging or use the following methods to explore the city:

- **Vaporetto (Water Bus):** The canals of Venice are home to a vast network of vaporettos that travel between different areas of the city. Vaporettos can be used to travel to your lodging or to discover new areas and activities.

- **Water Taxi**: You can book a water taxi to take you directly to your lodging or any desired location in Venice if you would rather have a more direct and private transfer. Water taxis can be hired in advance from hotels or taxi companies or found at designated taxi stations.

- **Walking**: Depending on how close your lodging is to the arrival location, walking might be a practical choice, particularly if you just have little bags. Venice is a city that encourages pedestrians, making it a pleasure to stroll through its streets.

It is advised to research the prices and timetables of the available transportation alternatives beforehand, particularly if you have set arrival or departure hours. To save time and guarantee a pleasant journey, think about obtaining travel passes or tickets beforehand.

Public Transportation in the City

The vaporetto, or water bus, is the main means of public transit in Venice. The city is connected to one another by a vast network of vaporettos that go along the canals. What you should know before riding a vaporetto in Venice is as follows:

- The Grand Canal, which runs through the centre of the city and offers a fantastic perspective of the palaces and historic structures, is one of the accessible routes. Murano and Burano are just two of the bridges that connect the lagoon's islands.

- **Tickets**: Vaporetto tickets can be bought from ticket booths, vending machines, or licensed dealers. You can make as many stops as you want during the 75-minute validity of a single ticket. If you want to use vaporettos frequently while visiting, you may also get multi-day passes.

- **Validation**: Before getting on the vaporetto, make sure to validate your ticket by tapping it on the reader. If inspectors see you breaking this rule, they may penalise you.

- Vaporetto schedules can change depending on the route and time of day, but they generally run on time. Before setting off on your journey, check the schedules.

- **Crowds**: During peak hours, particularly on popular routes, vaporettos may become congested. If the vaporetto is extremely crowded, be prepared to wait or stand.

A few alternative transit choices are available in Venice besides vaporettos:

- **Water taxis:** If you'd want a more direct and individualised transfer, you can hire private water taxis. Although they can be pricey, water taxis provide a useful and opulent service.

- **Gondolas**: Travelling around Venice's canals in a gondola is a classic and memorable experience. They are best used for brief, leisurely trips or romantic outings because they are typically more expensive than vaporettos or water taxis.

Overall, getting around Venice effectively and exploring the city may be accomplished by taking the public transit system. Just be sure to prepare for crowds at peak hours by planning your routes, getting valid tickets, and buying them.

Understanding the Vaporetto System

For effective city navigation in Venice, one must be familiar with the Vaporetto system. Here are some essential ideas to help you comprehend and utilise the Vaporetto system to its full potential:

- The Vaporetto system consists of a variety of numbered lines that go along various routes in Venice. Each route has specific stops along the canals so you can board and depart at different points.

- **Prominent Vaporetto Stops**: The main entrance to the city, Piazzale Roma, the train station, Rialto, San Marco, and Fondamente Nove are a few of the prominent Vaporetto stops in Venice. These stations typically have clear signage and act as significant transportation hubs.

- Schedules and route maps are accessible online or in travel guides in addition to being available at Vaporetto stops. The many lines, stations, and their corresponding routes are shown on the maps. It's beneficial to look at the maps in advance and note the stops and lines you'll require to get to your target locations.

- **Tickets for the Vaporetto:** Major Vaporetto stops have ticket booths, vending machines, or authorised resellers where you can buy tickets. Tickets may also be ordered in advance online.

You can make transfers during the 75-minute period that follows the time your single-journey tickets are validated. Consider buying a multi-day travel pass if you want to use Vaporettos a lot while you're there for limitless travel.

- In order to use your Vaporetto ticket, you must validate it by tapping it on the electronic card reader located at the entrance of the vehicle. If you are inspected by ticket inspectors for failing to do so, a fine may be assessed.

- Vaporetto frequencies might change depending on the line and the time of day. Peak hours are also a factor. Vaporettos often run throughout the day, but they are more prevalent during rush hours, particularly on major routes. During these times, expect crowds. Be ready for them.

- **Night Service:** The Vaporetto service is also available at night, however at lower frequencies than during the day. If you intend to use Vaporettos after hours, it is essential to check the schedules beforehand as some lines may have restricted or altered routes.

- **Accessibility:** Some Vaporetto stops and vessels are set up to accommodate those with disabilities or those who have trouble moving around. The ramps or lifts at these accessible stops and vessels make boarding and disembarking easier. On the Vaporetto maps, look for the accessibility emblem, and if you require assistance, ask at the stops.

You can travel Venice with ease and utilise this well-liked method of public transportation effectively by being familiar with the Vaporetto lines, maps, schedules, and ticketing system.

EXPLORING THE NEIGHBOURHOODS

The city of Venice is divided into several distinctive neighbourhoods, each of which has its allure, personality, and attractions. You'll have a better idea of the city's different options by exploring these neighbourhoods. The following notable areas are listed for your consideration:

- **San Marco**: The centre of Venice, St. Mark's Square (Piazza San Marco), is located in this district. Famous structures including St. Mark's Basilica, the Doge's Palace, and the Campanile can be found here. The region is renowned for its stunning architecture, high-end stores, and energetic atmosphere.

- One of Venice's biggest and most established neighbourhoods is Cannaregio. With its lovely canals, quaint squares, and secret passageways, it offers a more intimate and residential atmosphere. Don't forget to visit the world's oldest Jewish Ghetto, which you may explore while enjoying delectable Jewish-Italian cuisine.

- **Dorsoduro**: Known for its thriving arts community, Dorsoduro is the location of the Accademia Gallery, which holds an extraordinary collection of Venetian art, and the famed Peggy Guggenheim Collection. Additionally, this area has hip eateries, beautiful canal vistas, and a bohemian vibe. Consider taking a stroll along the waterfront on the picturesque Zattere promenade.

- **San Polo**: In the heart of Venice, there is a historic district called San Polo. One of the most recognizable monuments in the city is the Rialto Bridge, also known as the Ponte di Rialto. Discover the vibrant Rialto Market, where you can buy local goods, fresh seafood, and veggies. Many lovely churches and secret squares may be found in San Polo.

- The largest and most diversified area in Venice is called Castello, and it is renowned for its winding streets, tranquil canals, and friendly attitude. Visit the ancient Arsenal, which was once the biggest shipyard in Europe, and stroll through the calm side alleys to see quaint squares and regional artisan studios.

The famed Venice Biennale art show is housed in the Biennale Gardens, which you shouldn't miss.

- **Giudecca**: Across the Giudecca Canal from Venice's main island, Giudecca provides a quiet, residential haven away from the city's bustle. Visit the famous Church of the Redeemer (Chiesa del Santissimo Redentore), take in breathtaking views of the city skyline, and unwind in waterfront cafes.

  Giudecca also has a few opulent hotels and former industrial structures that hold cultural events.

- The island of Lido in Venice is a well-liked vacation spot recognized for its sand beaches and the Venice Film Festival. With hotels on the beach, eateries by the water, and bike routes, it provides a more laid-back and resort-like ambiance. Explore the lovely neighbourhoods on the island, take a stroll down the promenade, or relax on the beach.

Each district in Venice has a distinct vibe and attractions that make for a rich and varied experience. Spend some time wandering the streets, discovering new places, and getting to know the people, history, and natural beauty of this fascinating city.

San Marco

One of Venice's most well-known and recognizable neighbourhoods, San Marco is renowned for its magnificent architecture, important historical sites, and lively environment. What to anticipate when visiting San Marco is as follows:

- The majestic St. Mark's Square, also known as Piazza San Marco, is the centre of San Marco and is frequently referred to as the "drawing room of Europe." St. Mark's Basilica, the Doge's Palace, the Clock Tower (Torre dell'Orologio), and the Procuratie buildings are just a few of the magnificent structures that surround it.

With bustling eateries, live street performers, and a steady stream of visitors, the square is a centre of activity.

- San Marco's St. Mark's Basilica, also known as the Basilica di San Marco, is a stunning cathedral built in Byzantine style. Admire the elaborate embellishments, beautiful mosaics, and renowned Pala d'Oro altarpiece.

  Take your time looking around the interior and think about stepping up to the terrace for sweeping views of the square.

- The Doge's Palace, also known as the Palazzo Ducale, is a magnificent example of Venetian Gothic architecture and is situated next to St. Mark's Basilica. Visit the Doge's apartments, cross the Bridge of Sighs, and meander through the prisons that previously housed famous inmates in luxurious rooms. Additionally, the palace is home to many museums and art collections.

- **Campanile di San Marco**: The bell tower, which dominates the square, offers commanding views of Venice. Enjoy panoramic views of the city, its canals, and the far-off islands by taking the elevator to the top.

- **Museo Correr:** The Museo Correr, which is located on the southern edge of St. Mark's Square, provides a window into Venetian history, culture, and art. Discover works of art that captures the splendour of Venice's history, including paintings, sculptures, historical objects, and period chambers.

- **Procuratie Vecchie e Nuove**: St. Mark's Square is bordered by these opulent structures, which also house upmarket stores, cafes, and museums. Explore the fancy boutiques, stroll the colonnades, and enjoy some people-watching from the outdoor seating areas.

- **Cafés in the style of the Venetians**: San Marco is renowned for its old cafés, some of which have been in business for centuries. Take in the atmosphere of these legendary establishments while sipping on coffee or a classic Venetian beverage like the spritz.

- **Shopping**: There are upscale clothing businesses, excellent jewellery stores, and luxury boutiques in San Marco. Look around St. Mark's Square and the major retail street, Mercerie, for one-of-a-kind trinkets, Murano glass, and Venetian masks.

Undoubtedly, San Marco is a thriving and bustling district that displays the splendour and cultural legacy of Venice. Take your time to discover its treasures, acquaint yourself with the vibrant atmosphere, and admire the architectural wonders that contribute to this area's allure.

Cannaregio

In the northern region of Venice, there is a picturesque old area called Cannaregio. Cannaregio, which is well-known for its intimate ambiance, charming canals, and winding alleyways, provides a more genuine and residential feel. What you can find when you explore Cannaregio is as follows:

- **Jewish Ghetto:** One of the world's oldest Jewish ghettos is located in Cannaregio. Learn about Venice's Jewish community's rich history and cultural legacy by visiting the Jewish Museum. Explore the synagogues, eat at nearby kosher restaurants, and stroll through the historic neighbourhood's winding streets.

- The main street in Cannaregio is called Strada Nova, and it is crowded with local shops, cafes, and enterprises. It has a lively environment and is well-liked by both residents and tourists. Walk leisurely down this bustling street, look at the stores, and pause for a coffee or gelato.

- Fondamenta della Misericordia: Cannaregio's quaint seaside promenade is lined with eateries, cafés, and outdoor lounging places. It's a wonderful spot to eat, drink wine, and take in the passing boats. On the nights, the atmosphere is boisterous, making it a popular gathering place for both locals and visitors.

- Visit the Church of Santa Maria dei Miracoli, a stunning Renaissance building renowned for its ornate marble front and detailed interior. The church is a hidden treasure located in a peaceful area of Cannaregio and is attractive from an architectural standpoint.

- Explore the Venetian Ghetto Nuovo, one of the original neighbourhoods of the Jewish Ghetto. There are little squares, gorgeous canals, and winding lanes in this area of Cannaregio. It has a more serene atmosphere and provides an insight into local inhabitants' daily lives.

- **Ponte delle Guglie:** This charming bridge crosses the Cannaregio Canal and provides a beautiful perspective of the area. The bridge gets its name from the four towering, needle-like spires ("gurgle") that embellish it. Consider how lovely the canal and the nearby buildings are for a moment.

- **Campo dei Mori:** Learn about the intriguing history of this tiny plaza known as Campo dei Mori. The "Mori," or four statues, are depictions of Middle Eastern traders who once resided in Venice. Take in the tranquillity of the square while learning about its cultural significance.

You may discover a more intimate and residential aspect of Venice at Cannaregio. Embrace the town's genuineness, stroll through its quaint streets, and take in Cannaregio's illustrious past and vibrant present to fully appreciate this hidden gem of a neighbourhood.

Dorsoduro

A thriving area called Dorsoduro may be found in Venice's southern region. The neighbourhood of Dorsoduro, which is well-known for its artistic legacy, gorgeous canals, and bohemian vibe, offers a delightful fusion of history, culture, and charm. Here are some of the top attractions in Dorsoduro to check out:

- **Peggy Guggenheim Collection**: The Peggy Guggenheim Collection, which is located on the Grand Canal, is a must-see attraction for art lovers. It has a sizable collection of contemporary art, including pieces by well-known artists like Picasso, Pollock, and Dal.

  Take your time admiring the artwork and taking in the lovely garden with a canal view.

- **The Accademia Gallery (Gallerie dell'Accademia)** is home to a sizable collection of Venetian artwork from the 14th to the 18th century. It is housed in the former Scuola della Carità building. Admire the creations of well-known Venetian artists like Titian, Veronese, and Tintoretto to learn more about the history of the city's arts.

- **Squares in Dorsoduro:** Dorsoduro is home to several attractive squares where you may unwind, observe locals, and take in the ambiance.

A bustling centre with cafes and restaurants surrounding it, Campo Santa Margherita is frequented by locals and students. The peaceful neighbourhood of Campo Santo Stefano has a lovely church and close-by eateries.

- **Zattere Promenade:** The Giudecca Canal is bordered by a length of waterfront promenade known as the Zattere. Enjoy a stroll while taking in the panoramic views of the canal as you pass past old houses, churches, and coffee shops. It's a wonderful location to see Venice's serene splendour and the setting sun.

- Visit the Ca' Rezzonico, a magnificent mansion that today functions as a museum devoted to Venice in the eighteenth century. Discover the opulent spaces, take in the frescoes and antique furnishings, and learn about Venetian nobility at the height of the city's glory.

- Discover Squero di San Trovaso, one of Venice's last remaining classic gondola boatyards. Discover the skill required to preserve these iconic Venetian boats as you watch professional craftsmen build and repair gondolas by hand.

- **Campo San Barnaba:** This delightful square is well-known for the beautiful Chiesa di San Barnaba, which was portrayed in the motion picture "Indiana Jones and the Last Crusade." Enjoy the neighbourhood cafes and look around the handmade shops close by.

Dorsoduro is a fascinating neighbourhood to explore since it offers a combination of art, culture, and natural beauty. Dorsoduro will leave you with long-lasting recollections of Venice's creative legacy thanks to its top-notch museums, charming squares, and waterfront promenades.

Castello

In the eastern portion of Venice, there is a diversified and interesting district called Castello. Away from the hectic tourist hordes, Castello offers a more genuine and residential experience with its rich history, peaceful canals, and local atmosphere.

Highlights of what you can find when exploring Castello are listed below:

- **Arsenale:** The Arsenale is a historically noteworthy complex of shipyards that previously had a substantial impact on the nautical strength of Venice. Explore the region and take in the Arsenale buildings' stunning architecture.

    Even though there may not be much access to the interior, the grandeur is still visible from the outside.

- **Giardini della Biennale:** One of the most famous exhibitions of contemporary art in the world, the Venice Biennale, is held in this lovely park. Outside of the Biennale activities, guests can wander quietly through the park, unwind amidst the foliage, and take in numerous sculptures and installations.

- **Visit the San Pietro di Castello Cathedral**, which served as the former residence of the Patriarch of Venice. Admire the church's opulent interior, stunning Byzantine mosaics, and serene ambiance. You may also take in expansive views of the lake from the nearby Campo San Pietro.

- Explore the Church of San Zaccaria, which is renowned for its stunning Renaissance architecture and superb artwork. Admire the church's magnificent altarpieces, deft sculptures, and elaborate chapels.

- Walk down Via Garibaldi, a bustling street dotted with neighbourhood stores, cafes, and eateries. Wander through this bustling area of Castello and observe true Venetian daily life.

- Find out more about the Church of San Francesco della Vigna, which is renowned for its opulent façade and tranquil cloister. Enter to enjoy the artistic treasures, which include pieces by well-known Venetian painters.

- The scenic waterfront promenade known as Riva Schiavoni provides breathtaking views of the lagoon and the island of San Giorgio

Maggiore. Enjoy the marine ambiance while taking a leisurely stroll along the Riva degli Schiavoni and watching the gondolas and vaporettos pass by.

- Castello is full of undiscovered areas and secret gems just waiting to be found. Discover the small streets and secret squares of this delightful area as you stroll around and take in the local atmosphere.

Castello offers a more sedate and intimate atmosphere, giving visitors a chance to witness real Venetian life. Castello invites you to explore and find the hidden gems of this interesting neighbourhood, from historic landmarks to tranquil waterways.

Santa Croce

Santa Croce, a lovely district in the western region of Venice, is well-known for its quaint canals, antique structures, and neighbourhood feel. The following are some of the highlights of what can be seen at Santa Croce:

- One of the oldest churches in Venice is the stunning Church of San Giacomo dell'Orio, where you should begin your exploration. Admire the magnificent exterior before entering to see stunning artwork, including works by well-known Venetian painters.

- **Campo San Giacomo dell'Orio:** The centre of Santa Croce, this bustling piazza is where locals congregate. Sit at a café outside and take in the laid-back atmosphere while you watch Venice life go by.

- Visit the Fondaco dei Turchi, a historic structure that serves as the Venice Museum of Natural History. Investigate the displays highlighting the natural marvels and historical relics of the Venetian Republic.

- The magnificent Ca' Pesaro, a Baroque mansion that houses the Museum of Modern Art, is worth exploring. Discover the extensive collection of paintings, sculptures, and installations created by Italian and foreign artists in the 19th and 20th centuries.

- **Scuola Grande di San Rocco**: Be awed by the artistic riches housed within this majestic structure, which is decorated with superb paintings by Tintoretto. Explore the large collection of paintings that depict scenes from the Bible as well as the intricate ceiling frescoes.

- Cross the Ponte degli Scalzi, a bridge that connects Santa Croce with the Cannaregio area and spans the Grand Canal. Enjoy the expansive views of the canal and the exquisite buildings that line its banks.

- **Campo San Polo**: Leave Santa Croce's perimeter and visit the nearby Campo San Polo, one of Venice's biggest squares. Enjoy a leisurely stroll across this open area, the tranquillity, and possibly a nearby concert or event.

- **Hidden Calles and Canals**: Santa Croce is home to a number of charming canals and obscure alleyways. Discover the neighbourhood's true appeal by taking the time to stroll along the canals, over the lovely bridges, and explore the tiny passageways.

With its lovely squares, ancient structures, and undiscovered nooks, Santa Croce offers a more sedate and residential experience in Venice. Take in the neighbourhood vibe, admire the stunning architecture, and experience the real Venetian way of life Santa Croce has to offer.

TOP ATTRACTIONS IN VENICE

Venice is a beautiful city with many famous landmarks and amazing attractions. The following are some of the top Venice attractions you shouldn't skip:

- Piazza San Marco, also known as St. Mark's Square, is the centre of Venice and is a bustling square surrounded by beautiful buildings. Discover the exquisite mosaics inside St. Mark's Basilica and climb the Campanile for sweeping views of the city.

- Explore the beautiful Doge's Palace (Palazzo Ducale), a representation of Venetian power and authority. Admire the lavish spaces, cross the Bridge of Sighs, and discover the background of the Venetian Republic.

- Cross the historic Rialto Bridge (Ponte di Rialto), one of Venice's most recognizable monuments. Enjoy the Grand Canal vistas, stroll through the lively Rialto Market, and look around the shops selling regional handicrafts and mementos.

- Take a vaporetto (water bus) journey down Venice's principal waterway, the Grand Canal. Enjoy the majestic palaces and structures that flank the canal as you take in the distinctive ambiance of this busy waterway.

- Visit the Peggy Guggenheim Collection, a well-known gallery featuring contemporary art. Explore the artwork of Picasso, Pollock, and Dali while taking in the lovely garden with views of the Grand Canal.

- Constructed to connect the Doge's Palace with the prison, the Bridge of Sighs (Ponte dei Sospiri) is a stunning and well-known bridge. According to legend, the bridge gained its name from captives' sighs as they saw their final glimpse of Venice.

- **Santa Maria della Salute:** Take in the splendour of this magnificent basilica, which is situated at the start of the Grand Canal. Wander about the church, take in the serene ambiance, and take in the breathtaking views of the ocean.

Visit the Gallerie dell'Accademia, which has a sizable collection of Venetian artwork from the 14th to the 18th century. Admire masterpieces by artists like Titian, Veronese, and Tintoretto, among others, and learn about Venice's rich artistic history.

- Take a boat ride to Murano Island, which is renowned for its glassmaking traditions. Visit glass factories to see how expert craftsmen make exquisite glass pieces. Don't pass up the chance to get one-of-a-kind Murano glass keepsakes.

- Visit Burano Island, which is renowned for its vibrant homes and lace-making history. Learn about the meticulous lace artistry that has been handed down through the years as you stroll through the lively streets and observe the gorgeous canals.

These are just a few of the main attractions that contribute to Venice's allure. Explore the city's historical monuments, artistic gems, and quaint districts as you embrace its beauty and distinctiveness.

St. Mark's Square and Basilica

Two of the most famous and important landmarks in Venice are St. Mark's Basilica and St. Mark's Square (Piazza San Marco). What you should know about these amazing landmarks is as follows:

Piazza San Marco, also known as St. Mark's Square

- The principal open space in Venice is St. Mark's Square, which is situated at the eastern part of the city.

- Due to its historical and cultural significance, it is frequently referred to as the "drawing room of Europe".

- St. Mark's Basilica, the Doge's Palace, the Procuratie buildings, and the recognizable Clock Tower

(Torre dell'Orologio) are just a few of the spectacular architectural landmarks that surround the square.

- For centuries, St. Mark's Square has served as the centre of social, political, and religious life in Venice.

- Both locals and visitors frequent the square, which has a bustling environment thanks to street performers, cafes, and businesses.

The Basilica of St. Mark (Basilica di San Marco):

- The most well-known church in Venice and one of the world's best examples of Byzantine architecture is St. Mark's Basilica.

- It serves as the cathedral for the Archdiocese of Venice and is situated on the eastern side of St. Mark's Square.

- The church displays the wealth and authority of the Venetian Republic with magnificent domes, dexterous mosaics, and marble columns.

- The basilica's interior is beautiful and features golden mosaics of biblical subjects, exquisite Byzantine artwork, and the Pala d'Oro, a glittering altarpiece set with priceless stones.

- Don't forget to stop by the Museo Marciano to discover more about the history and artwork of the basilica as well as the Treasury to see a collection of holy relics.

Visitor advice for the Basilica and St. Mark's Square:

- To avoid the crowds and have a more relaxing experience, arrive early in the morning or late in the evening.

- Be respectful and wear modest clothing because the basilica is a sacred space. Inside the church, caps must be taken off and shoulders and knees must be covered.

- To discover more about the St. Mark's Basilica's history, artwork, and architectural elements, think about going on a guided tour.

- Spend some time exploring the basilica's façade and interior, taking in the ornate features and magnificent mosaics.

- To get a bird's-eye view of St. Mark's Square and the surrounding area, climb the Campanile (bell tower). Amazing views may be seen from the top.

- The Basilica and St. Mark's Square should definitely be visited when in Venice. Enjoy these famous sites' fascinating histories, breathtaking architecture, and artistic splendour, which have come to represent Venice's very best.

Doge's Palace

Venice's Doge's Palace (Palazzo Ducale) is a stunning piece of architecture and a significant historical site. What you should know about this gorgeous palace is as follows:

Overview:

- The Doge's Palace is situated next to St. Mark's Basilica at the eastern end of St. Mark's Square.

- It served as the venue for the executive and judicial branches of the Venetian Republic's government as well as the house of the elected Doge of Venice.

- The palace, which combines Byzantine, Moorish, and Renaissance elements, is a beautiful example of Venetian Gothic architecture.

- It serves as a representation of Venetian riches, power, and the city's extensive cultural legacy.

Highlights:

- Explore the inner courtyard and the arcaded loggia, which both have beautiful columns and arches, to start your stay.

- The magnificent staircase, known as the Scala dei Giganti (Giant's Staircase), which leads to the palace's ceremonial halls is embellished with statues of Mars and Neptune.

- Discover the exquisitely painted chambers where the various institutions of the Venetian Republic did business in the Institutional Chambers tour. These include the Senate Hall, the Council of Ten, the Great Council

Chamber, and the Chamber of Quarantia's Council.

- Explore the private quarters of the Doge and his family, which are filled with priceless artwork, opulent furnishings, and elaborate decorations, in the Doge's Apartments.

- Cross the renowned Bridge of Sighs (Ponte dei Sospiri), which connects the Doge's Palace to the New Prison. The bridge has a charming legend attached to it and provides lovely views of the canal.

- **Prisons and Piombi**: Make your way down to the jail quarters under the palace. Learn about jail life in the Venetian Republic by touring the Piombi, the notorious cells in the attic.

Advice for travelling to Doge's Palace:

- If you want to skip the wait and make the most of your visit, think about buying a skip-the-line ticket or scheduling a guided tour in advance.

- You can obtain comprehensive information and historical background about the palace through audio guides or guided tours.

- Explore each area at your leisure, savour the artwork, and take in the architectural features.

- Keep an eye out for noteworthy artwork, such as masterpieces by artists like Tintoretto, Veronese, and Bellini.
- For stunning views of St. Mark's Square, the Grand Canal, and the

Venice skyline, visit the rooftop terraces.

- Before making travel arrangements, confirm the opening times and any restrictions as there might occasionally be closures or access restrictions to specific palace areas.

- A unique look into Venice's political, historical, and aesthetic legacy can be found at the Doge's Palace. Explore this magnificent palace's luxurious halls, traverse the Bridge of Sighs, and learn about the prosperous Venetian Republic as you become engrossed in its magnificence.

Rialto Bridge and Market

One of Venice's most recognizable and well-liked tourist attractions is the Rialto Market. What you should know about these well-known landmarks is as follows:

Overview:

- The San Marco and San Polo neighbourhoods are connected by the stone arch Rialto Bridge, which spans the Grand Canal.

- With a history that dates back to the 16th century, it is one of the most illustrious and historic bridges in Venice.

- A variety of fresh vegetables, seafood, and souvenirs are available at the nearby Rialto Market, one of Venice's biggest and oldest markets.

Highlights:

- Take a leisurely stroll across the Rialto Bridge to take in the breathtaking views of the Grand Canal and the nearby buildings. The bridge is especially lovely after dusk and in the morning when there are fewer people around.

- **Rialto Market**: To enjoy the lively ambiance of a genuine Venetian market, go to the Rialto Market. Try some of the locally produced fresh fruits, vegetables, fish, and treats like tramezzini and cicchetti, which are little sandwiches.

- Discover the old Mercato di Rialto market building, which is close to the bridge. The structure was constructed in the 16th century and has a remarkable Venetian Gothic design.

- **Ponte di Rialto:** From one of the numerous gondolas or water taxis that pass underneath the bridge, take in the picturesque views of the Grand Canal. Both the vista from the bridge itself and the view from the water are stunning.

Visitor advice for the Rialto Bridge and Market

- Visit the Rialto Market early in the day when it is most active and lively. The market is open from 7 am till 1 pm.

- Since many of the merchants at the market do not accept credit cards, bring cash with you.

- Consider going early in the morning or late in the evening to avoid the busiest times and be prepared for crowds.

- To find out more about the background and traditions of Venetian food and regional delicacies, think about joining a market trip.

- Take your time and stroll around the neighbourhood, taking in the nearby churches, plazas, and museums.

- Take lots of pictures to document the splendour and atmosphere of this famous Venetian site.

- The Rialto Bridge and Market provide visitors a taste of Venice's thriving history, culture, and cuisine. The Rialto Bridge and Market should not be missed whether sightseeing, shopping, or dining are on your list of interests.

Grand Canal

The main canal that runs through the centre of Venice is called the Grand Canal. One of the most recognizable and beautiful aspects of the city is it. What you should know about the Grand Canal is as follows:

Overview:

- The Grand Canal, or Canal Grande in Italian, is a huge S-shaped waterway that runs the length of Venice for roughly 3.8 kilometres (2.4 miles).

- It is the city's principal roadway and the primary route for vaporettos (water buses), water taxis, boats, and gondolas.

- The San Marco and Dorsoduro districts are located on one side of the canal, and San Polo and Santa Croce are located on the other.

- There are many spectacular palaces, old structures, and charming bridges along the Grand Canal's banks.

Highlights:

- **Palaces and Architecture**: The Grand Canal is lined with magnificent palaces and structures that highlight the Venetian city's architectural splendour. Ca' d'Oro, Palazzo Barbaro, Palazzo Dario, and Palazzo Contarini-Fasan are a few noteworthy landmarks.

- **Rialto Bridge:** The Rialto Bridge, one of Venice's most recognizable bridges, spans the Grand Canal and provides sweeping panoramas of the waterway and its surroundings.

- **Vaporetto Ride:** One of the best ways to see Venice's allure and beauty is to take a vaporetto ride around the Grand Canal. As you cruise along the waterway, take a seat back, unwind, and take in the beautiful scenery.

- **Promenades along the Canals:** Take in the ambience by strolling along the fondamenta, or canal-side promenades. Discover the hidden gems and neighbourhood stores amid the winding alleyways and alleys that border the Grand Canal.

How to navigate the Grand Canal:

- For a different perspective of the city, take a vaporetto trip along the Grand Canal. The widely used Vaporetto Line 1 spans the entire length of the canal and makes stops at a number of stations.

- To get closer to the palaces and structures along the canal, think about going on a tour in a boat or a romantic ride in a gondola.

- Visit the Rialto Bridge and take in the scenery from both the bridge and the surrounding Rialto Market.

- Discover secret nooks and regional treasures by exploring the minor canals and side alleys that branch out from the Grand Canal.

- Utilise the numerous viewing points along the canal to take beautiful pictures of the recognizable Venetian landscape.

- The Grand Canal serves as a crucial thoroughfare for transit as well as a representation of Venice's distinctive and alluring personality. As you go through the centre of the city, take in the beauty and grace of this spectacular canal and let yourself be enchanted by the stunning architecture that surrounds it.

Peggy Guggenheim Collection

In Venice, Italy, there is a renowned art gallery called The Peggy Guggenheim Collection. What you should know about this special museum is as follows:

Overview:

- The Palazzo Venier dei Leoni, an incomplete 18th-century mansion situated on the Grand Canal in the Dorsoduro neighbourhood of Venice, serves as the home of the Peggy Guggenheim Collection.

- Peggy Guggenheim, a prominent American art patron and collector, exhibits her own art collection in the museum.

- The collection's main focus is 20th-century modern art, which includes pieces by well-known painters such Pablo Picasso, Jackson Pollock, Salvador Dali, and Wassily Kandinsky.

- The gallery is renowned for its superb collection of American and European avant-garde artwork, which includes Cubist, Surrealist, and Abstract Expressionist pieces.

Highlights:

- Paintings, sculptures, and works on paper are just a few of the artworks in the Peggy Guggenheim Collection. Visitors can explore various artistic movements and styles while admiring works of art created by well-known artists.

- The museum is located in a striking palazzo that was formerly Peggy Guggenheim's home, the Palazzo Venier dei Leoni. A unique art experience is offered by the palace's exclusive and intimate atmosphere.

- **Sculpture Garden**: The museum is home to a stunning outdoor sculpture garden where guests may unwind and take in the artworks in a natural environment. The garden provides a tranquil haven in the busy metropolis of Venice.

- **Temporary Exhibitions**: The museum presents temporary exhibitions that feature contemporary and modern art from a range of movements and artists in addition to its permanent collection.

Visitor recommendations for the Peggy Guggenheim Collection:

- Check the museum's hours of operation and think about buying tickets in advance to prevent excessive lines, especially during the busiest travel times.

- Explore the artworks at your own pace and at your own time. There are guided tours and audio guides that can provide you with more information about the collection.

- The outdoor sculpture park, which offers a serene atmosphere and breathtaking views of the Grand Canal, should not be missed.

- To experience the museum in a distinctive and lively atmosphere, think of going during special events or exhibition openings.

- Utilise the museum store, which provides a variety of art publications, prints, and mementos.

- For people who enjoy art and are interested in modern and contemporary art, the Peggy Guggenheim Collection is a must-see location. Explore this magnificent museum and its outstanding collection in the picturesque city of Venice and immerse yourself in the colourful world of 20th-century art.

BEYOND THE MUST-SEE SIGHTS

While Venice is famous for its well-known attractions, there are still undiscovered treasures and undiscovered nooks that provide a distinctive and genuine experience. Here are some suggestions for venturing beyond the must-see attractions:

- **Giudecca Island:** Take a vaporetto to Giudecca Island to avoid the throng. Take in the calm ambiance, wander along the waterfront promenade, and stop by the Church of the Redeemer for breathtaking city views.

- **Islands in the Venetian Lagoon:** Take a tour of the islands of Murano, Burano, and Torcello. Burano is well-known for its colourful homes and lace-making, while Torcello provides an insight into Venice's early history. Murano is well-known for its legacy of glassmaking.

- Visit the Fondaco dei Tedeschi, an ancient structure close to the Rialto Bridge. It now functions as a posh shopping mall, but it also includes a breathtaking rooftop terrace with sweeping views of Venice.

- **Scuola Grande di San Rocco:** Explore the spectacular Scuola Grande di San Rocco, which is adorned with complex works of art by Tintoretto. Explore the numerous chambers of this little-known treasure and take in the breathtaking ceiling frescoes.

- Discover the historical Jewish Ghetto of Venice, the first ghetto ever built. Discover the history of

Venice's Jewish community, see the synagogues, and take in the quaint alleyways and boutiques.

- **Libreria Acqua Alta:** Enter the unusual Libreria Acqua Alta, a bookstore with book-filled gondolas, stairs made of books, and heaps of books. For book enthusiasts and those looking for a special experience, it is a distinctive and endearing location.

- Visit the church and bell tower on San Giorgio Maggiore Island after a quick boat ride there. For spectacular panoramas of Venice's skyline, climb the bell tower.

- **Sestiere Castello:** Take a stroll through Castello's less-visited neighbourhood to find its winding streets, neighbourhood markets, and secret plazas. Away from the bustle, visit the Church of San

Francesco della Vigna and take in the tranquil environment.

- **Lido di Venezia:** Take a break on this barrier island for lovely beaches and a more laid-back attitude. Take a stroll along the promenade that runs along the ocean or go swimming in the Adriatic.

- **Local Food Experiences:** Savour Venice's delectable cuisine outside of the tourist hubs. Visit the authentic bacari (wine bars) that residents visit in the Cannaregio neighbourhood to sample traditional cicchetti (Venetian tapas) and regional wine.

You can gain a more thorough and genuine insight into Venice's culture, history, and everyday life by straying off the beaten path and discovering these hidden jewels. Discover the riches that lie beyond the must-see attractions by embracing the spirit of discovery.

The Island of Venice: Torcello, Burano, and Murano

The Venetian Lagoon's islands of Murano, Burano, and Torcello provide a wonderful diversion from Venice's busy streets. Every island has a distinct charm and charms of its own. What to anticipate to find on these alluring islands is as follows:

- **Murano**: Known for its long history of glassmaking, Murano is known for its fine glasswork.

- Visit glass factories to see how expert craftsmen use age-old methods to produce intricate works of glass art.

- Learn about the origins and development of Murano's glass industry by visiting the Murano Glass Museum.

- Don't pass up the chance to purchase exquisite glass mementos, such as delicate jewellery and ornate chandeliers.

- **Burano**: This gorgeous island, which is well-known for its brightly coloured homes, will enchant you right away.

- Explore the canals while admiring the colourful, vivid architecture.

- Burano is renowned for its history of producing lace. Discover the complex craft of making lace by going to the Lace Museum.

- At one of the area's seafood restaurants, take your time and eat classic delicacies in a charming environment.

- Torcello: The oldest and most serene of the three islands,

Torcello provides a window into the early history of Venice.

- Discover the magnificent mosaics and tranquil grounds of the historic church known as the Cathedral of Santa Maria Assunta.

- Discover the history, archeological discoveries, and artistic heritage of the island at the Museo di Torcello.

- Take a tranquil stroll through the island's trails to take in the tranquil setting and breathtaking scenery.

Advice for travellers to the islands:

- Consider purchasing a vaporetto (water transport) ticket that includes all three islands, or a day pass.

- There is a lot to see and discover on each island, so schedule enough time there during your vacation.

- Take a stop at a nearby café and savour some authentic Venetian delights like "file" (little fried dough balls) from Murano or Burano's colourful "bussolai" cookies.

- To understand more about the background, customs, and craftsmanship of these islands, think about joining a guided tour.

- The crowded alleys of Venice are a lovely contrast to the islands of Murano, Burano, and Torcello. Each island has its distinct charm, from the artistic glassmaking of Murano to the colourful buildings of Burano and the serenity of Torcello. Travel to these alluring islands to experience their natural beauty, rich history, and unique culture.

Lido Di Venezia

A barrier island in the Venetian Lagoon, Lido di Venezia, sometimes known as Lido, is only a short boat trip from the historic district of Venice. What you should know about Lido di Venezia is as follows:

- **Beaches**: Lido is a well-liked vacation spot for sunbathers and beach lovers because of its stunning sandy beaches.

- Lido Beach (Spiaggia del Lido), the primary beach area, spans along the eastern half of the island and provides amenities such as beach clubs, umbrellas, and sun loungers.

- Take advantage of the relaxing Mediterranean climate, soak up the sun, and cool down in the Adriatic Sea.

- Historic Hotels and Architecture: Lido is home to several historic hotels, including the renowned Hotel Excelsior and Hotel Des Bains, which have hosted famous visitors over the years.

- The main promenade, known as Gran Viale Santa Maria Elisabetta, is lined with exquisite Art Nouveau and Belle Époque buildings that exhibit the island's elegant early 20th-century architecture.

- One of the oldest and most famous film festivals in the world, the Venice Film Festival is held in Lido di Venezia.

- Every year in late August or early September, the festival draws to the island international actors, directors, and business leaders.

- You might get to enjoy the thrill and glitz of this renowned event if you go while the festival is going on.

- **Outdoor Activities**: In addition to its beaches, Lido also provides opportunities for biking, running, and walking along its lovely tree-lined boulevards.

- Take a stroll along the waterfront promenade while taking in views of the lagoon and the distant Venice cityscape, or rent a bicycle to explore the island's more tranquil side.

- **Local Venues & Restaurants**: The local environment in Lido is vibrant, with a wide range of eateries, cafés, and retail establishments that serve both locals and tourists.

- Experience mouthwatering seafood delicacies, and classic Italian dishes, or indulge in gelato while taking in the laid-back island vibe.

- Bars, clubs, and theatres are just a few of the entertainment options available in Lido.

Visitor advice for Lido di Venezia

- From the main island of Venice, take a vaporetto (water bus) to Lido. The trip takes about 15 to 20 minutes and has beautiful scenery along the way.

- To discover the island's quieter sections and secret nooks, think about renting a bike.

- While the island may be busier than normal if you visit during the Venice Film Festival, it's also an amazing time to experience the festival's buzz.

- If you intend to spend time at the beach, remember to bring your beach basics, such as sunscreen and swimsuit.

- Lido di Venezia offers a welcome respite from the bustle of the city's historic centre. With its distinctive fusion of natural beauty and cultural amenities, Lido offers a nice vacation whether you're looking for beach relaxation, magnificent architecture, or delicious local cuisine.

Giudecca

A small island called Giudecca is situated in the Venetian Lagoon, close to Venice's old city. It is a well-liked attraction for both locals and tourists because of its peaceful atmosphere and magnificent views of the city. What to anticipate when travelling to Giudecca is as follows:

- **Redentore Church:** The famous Redentore Church is a well-known landmark on the island. This stunning church, built by Andrea Palladio, is distinguished by its unusual dome and has an annual festival in July to mark the end of the plague.

- Giudecca is peppered with magnificent palazzi and houses that highlight the island's stunning architecture. You'll see a number of old structures as you stroll through its streets, reflecting the island's illustrious past and regal past.

- **Fondamenta delle Zitelle**: Enjoy a leisurely stroll along this waterfront promenade that provides breathtaking views of Venice's skyline. This beautiful walkway offers a peaceful retreat from the busy city bustle.

- **Restaurants & Cafés**: Giudecca has a wide selection of restaurants, from upmarket eateries to classic trattorias. relish the tranquil atmosphere of the island while indulging in delectable Venetian food.

- Giudecca is home to a number of art studios and workshops where you can watch regional artisans create one-of-a-kind works of art. These creative areas offer a window into the island's cultural legacy, from glassblowing to painting.

- **Local Life:** Compared to Venice's main island, Giudecca offers a stronger sense of neighbourhood and a more residential atmosphere. You may get a feel for island life as you walk the streets and pass by community squares, small food stores, and local shops.

- **Peaceful Retreat**: Giudecca provides a more serene and uncrowded alternative to Venice's busy neighbourhoods. It's the perfect location to avoid the crowds of tourists and take in a more laid-back, authentic Venetian experience.

- You may take a vaporetto (water bus) to Giudecca from a number of points in Venice, including San

Marco or Zattere. The trip offers the chance to take in the stunning views of the city and lagoon.

Giudecca offers a charming and genuine experience away from the busy streets of Venice, whether you're looking for picturesque vistas, a quiet refuge, or a taste of local life.

Venetian Villas On the Mainland

On the mainland surrounding Venice, there are numerous old country homes known as Venetian Villas. During the height of the Venetian Republic, affluent Venetian families constructed these beautiful homes as getaways for the summer.

Many of these villas are now accessible to the general public, allowing people to take in their exquisite architecture, verdant gardens, and historical significance. A few noteworthy Venetian villas on the mainland are listed below:

- A prominent example of Venetian Baroque architecture, Villa Pisani (Strà) is one of the most well-known Venetian villas. It is situated in the municipality of Strà.

- The home features magnificent frescoes, elaborate stucco accents, and a sizable garden with winding paths and fountains.

- The National Museum of Villa Pisani, which showcases historical items and works of art, is also housed there.

- **Villa Foscari (Malcontenta):** Villa Foscari, also known as La Malcontenta, is a famous villa created by renowned architect Andrea Palladio. It is located in the small community of Malcontenta.

- Palladian architectural traits, including a central portico and symmetrical design, are seen on the villa's façade.

- Visitors can view the villa from the outside and recognize its architectural value even though it is not accessible to the general public.

- A further masterpiece by Andrea Palladio is Villa Emo, which is located in Fanzolo di Vedelago.

- Palladio's distinctive style is evident in this Renaissance villa's balanced proportions, classical accents, and exquisite loggias.

- The villa, which is encircled by lovely grounds, provides guided tours so that visitors can explore its interior and discover its history.

- Villa Barbaro (Maser): Another masterpiece of Palladio's architecture can be found in the town of Maser.

- It is well known for the famous Italian painter Paolo Veronese's frescoes, which show scenes from mythology, history, and daily life.

- The villa is accessible to the general public, enabling guests to take in its exquisite artistic and architectural features.

These are only a few of the numerous Venetian villas that may be found on the mainland close to Venice. Visitors can learn about the lavish lifestyle of the Venetian nobles and gain an appreciation for the area's artistic and cultural legacy by touring these homes.

Venetian Cuisine and Local Restaurants

The wonderful flavour fusion of Venetian food is a result of its seaside setting, old trading routes, and regional products. Here is a description of Venetian gastronomy, including some of the region's best restaurants and seafood specialties:

- **Seafood specialties**: Due to Venice's proximity to the Adriatic Sea, seafood is a significant component of the regional cuisine. Be on the lookout for meals like risotto al nero di seppia (squid ink rice), fritto misto (mixed fried seafood), and sarde in saor (marinated sardines).

- **Bacari & Cicchetti:** In the traditional Venetian bars known as bacari, cicchetti are little, bite-sized nibbles traditionally savoured with a glass of wine.

Crostini with varied toppings, fried fish, and marinated veggies are a few examples. Don't pass up the chance to participate in a cicchetti crawl, when you hop from one bacaro to another while eating various treats.

- **Bigoli & pasta**: Made from whole wheat flour, bigoli is a traditional Venetian pasta that is frequently paired with heavy sauces like ragù or anchovy sauce. For a genuine flavour of Venetian pasta, look for places that serve handcrafted bigoli.

- Fegato alla veneziana, often known as Venetian-style liver, is a traditional meal made with sautéed calf liver and onions. It frequently functions as the main course and goes well with polenta.

- **Risi e Bisi:** A risotto-like typical Venetian dish, risi e bisi blends rice and peas. It is frequently served in many neighbourhood trattorias during the right season and is typically made with fresh spring peas.

Local eateries:

- Osteria Bancogiro: This eatery, which is close to the Rialto Bridge, offers a picturesque canal-side location and a menu of traditional Venetian foods with a contemporary twist.

- Osteria Alle Testiere is a quaint, intimate eatery renowned for its superb seafood dishes and friendly service. Due to its popularity, reservations are advised.

- The traditional Burano restaurant Trattoria da Romano is well known for its seafood delicacies, especially the risotto de g (grey mullet risotto).

- Cafe La Zucca: This osteria, a vegetarian-friendly choice in Venice, delivers inventive meals made with top-quality regional ingredients. meals with pumpkin are particularly well-liked here.

These are just a few of the various eateries and culinary experiences Venice has to offer. Immersing yourself in the local gastronomy and culture requires that you sample the cuisine of the area. Make sure to appreciate Venice's distinctive tastes and culinary customs.

ENJOYING VENETIAN CULTURE

Not only is Venice renowned for its beautiful architecture and scenic canals, but also for its extensive cultural history. Here are a few ideas for soaking up Venetian culture and making the most of your trip:

- Attend a session or go to a mask-making studio to learn about the craft of manufacturing Venetian masks. Make your mask or simply awe at the exquisite artistry that went into making these well-known Carnival emblems in Venice.

- Opera and Classical Music: In Venice, immerse yourself in the captivating world of opera and classical music. For a chance to see the works of great composers in a very magnificent setting, go to a concert at one of the city's ancient venues, like La Fenice Opera House.

- Visit the island of Murano, where glassblowing has a long history, for a taste of Venetian culture. To fully appreciate this exceptional art form, observe skilled glassblowers at work in their workshops, visit glass galleries, and possibly even take part in a glassblowing demonstration.

- **Historical Venetian Palaces:** Take a tour of a few of Venice's great palaces, many of which have been turned into museums or other cultural centres. To learn more about Venetian history, art, and architecture, go to places like Ca' Rezzonico, Palazzo Grassi, or Palazzo Ducale (Doge's Palace).

- **Venetian Cuisine:** Indulge in the flavours of Venetian food by trying out the regional trattorias' specialties. Enjoy cicchetti (snacks), local delicacies like risotto and sarde in saor, and fresh fish. Consider enrolling in a cooking course to learn how to make Venetian cuisine.

- **Venetian Festivals and Events:** To fully experience the culture, schedule your trip around one of Venice's vivacious festivals or events. The Feast of the Redeemer, the Historical Regatta, and the Venice Carnival are just a few of the fascinating events that happen all year long.

- **Explore Local Neighbourhoods:** To get a feel for the culture and way of life in the area, stroll through some of Venice's many neighbourhoods like Cannaregio, Dorsoduro, and Castello. To learn more about the customs and daily activities of the Venetians, visit local markets, peruse boutique stores, and converse with locals.

- **Venetian Gondola Ride:** Enjoy a leisurely gondola ride along Venice's canals, a must-do activity that enables you to take in the city's distinct ambiance and see its stunning architecture from a new angle.

Before your visit, don't forget to check the timetables and availability of particular cultural events or activities because some may demand reservations in advance or have limited availability. You'll forge enduring memories and forge a stronger bond with this magnificent city by immersing yourself in Venetian culture.

Festivals and Events

The colourful festivals and events that Venice hosts serve to highlight the city's extensive cultural legacy. The following are a few of the most well-liked festivals and events to attend in Venice:

- **Venice Carnival (Carnevale di Venezia):** One of the most renowned and ornate festivities in the world, the Venice Carnival is held in the weeks preceding Lent. It includes a range of events, such as masquerade balls and live performances, as well as parades, colourful costumes, and masks.

- **Venice Biennale:** Every two years, a renowned international art show called the Venice Biennale is held. It includes exhibitions, installations, performances, and cultural activities presented in various locations throughout the city and features modern art from all over the world.

- This annual rowing contest, which takes place on the first Sunday in September and is known as the "Historical Regatta," honours Venice's extensive nautical history. It includes a parade of vintage boats, gondoliers dressed in period attire, and exciting rowing contests along the Grand Canal.

- **Festa del Redentore**: The Redeemer Festival is a religious celebration that takes place on the third Sunday in July. Along with a spectacular fireworks show across the lagoon, a customary regatta, and boat processions, it honours the end of the plague in Venice.

- Filmmakers, actors, and other industry professionals from all over the world attend the Venice Film Festival (Mostra Internazionale d'Arte Cinematografica), one of the oldest film festivals in existence. It features a broad range of foreign films and is held every year in late August or early September.

- Reenactments of historical events that took place in Venice can be seen all year long. These events bring the city's past to life. These celebrations frequently feature historical-costumed processions, traditional music, and shows that reenact pivotal periods in the city's past.

- **Feast Days and Local Celebrations:** Throughout the year, a variety of feast days and local festivities are organised to celebrate patron saints, significant occasions in history, or regional customs. These occasions frequently feature musical performances, religious processions, and special food offerings.

It's crucial to keep in mind that some events might have set dates or alternate between various years, so it's a good idea to check the most recent information and event calendars for the set dates of the festivals and events you're interested in attending.

You may fully experience Venice's unique culture and customs by taking part in these festivals and events, which will make your trip even more memorable.

Classical Music and Opera

Venice has a long history as a centre for opera and classical music, and it still is. Here are some features and locations in Venice where you may hear opera and classical music:

- **La Fenice Opera House:** One of Italy's most well-known opera houses, Teatro La Fenice is a magnificent location that has played host to several historic performances and world premieres. Any fan of classical music must come here to see an opera or concert.

- Opera in an intimate environment can be enjoyed at Musica a Palazzo. The audience can go from room to room and interact closely with the actors because performances are held across numerous old palaces in the Venice area.

- In the old San Vidal Church, the chamber orchestra Interpreti Veneziani plays classical and Baroque music. The passionate performances of Interpreti Veneziani offer a great evening of classical music while showcasing the skills of nearby musicians.

- The Venice Baroque Orchestra was established by renowned violinist Andrea Marcon and is recognized for its faithful renditions of Baroque music. They frequently play in famous locations around the world, including Venice.

- The Chiesa di San Vidal, which is close to the Accademia Bridge, regularly hosts classical music performances. The church's acoustics make it the perfect location for solo and chamber music recitals.

- **Performances honouring Antonio Vivaldi:** The renowned composer was born in Venice, and you may attend performances honouring his music in several locations throughout the city. These performances frequently include accomplished musicians playing well-known works by Vivaldi, such as "The Four Seasons."

- Venice has several music festivals throughout the year, including the Settembre Musica Festival and the Venice Music Biennale. These concerts feature a wide range of classical music performances and modern compositions, bringing together renowned players.

Check the schedules and availability of performances at the various locations before your visit to make sure they are available. Especially in busy seasons, some concerts and operas might demand reservations in advance.

A classical music concert or opera in Venice offers the chance to take in the cultural legacy of the city and take in world-class performances in storied and evocative venues.

Venetian Mask-Making

Making Venetian masks is a traditional art form that has long been a part of Venice's cultural legacy. The history of the city is greatly influenced by the masks, especially during the yearly Carnival celebrations.

Here is a description of Venetian mask-making and some information on how to learn more about it:

- Venetian masks have a long history that dates back to the thirteenth century. The Venetian elite originally used masks to conceal their identity and participate in anonymous activities during the Carnival season. Masks were an integral aspect of Venetian culture and celebrations as mask wearing spread over time.

- **Traditional Mask-Making Methods:** Glassblowing, clay modelling, and papier-mâché are a few of the methods used to create Venetian masks. The most popular type of mask is called a papier-mâché mask, and it is manufactured by laying strips of paper over a mould before painting and embellishing it.

  Each mask is painstakingly hand-painted by artisans, who add exquisite details and brilliant colours.

- **Visiting Mask-Making Studios:** In Venice, you may visit mask-making studios and workshops to learn more about the Venetian mask-making process. These businesses provide workshops and demonstrations where you may learn about the processes and background of mask-making. Participants get hands-on experience making their own masks with the help of skilled artisans.

- Consider enrolling in a mask-making workshop to learn more about the skill. These courses often last a few hours or even many days and give you the chance to work with professional mask builders to master different techniques and design your own special mask.

- Examining Exhibitions on Mask Making: Venice organises exhibitions on masks where you may take in the workmanship and discover the various types and designs. These shows feature a wide range of masks, including classic Carnival masks and modern designs, and frequently offer historical context.

- **Carnival festivities:** Attending the Venice Carnival is the ideal way to experience the exquisite variety and beauty of Venetian masks. The city comes alive with people dressed in elaborate masks and costumes during the Carnival season.

You can take part in the celebrations, go to masquerade balls, and gaze in awe at the magnificent masks worn by both residents and guests.
- Making Venetian masks is a fascinating art form that lets you experience the city's inventiveness and cultural legacy. This experience offers a singular window into the enchanted world of Venetian Carnival traditions, whether you opt to make your own mask, visit workshops, or simply gaze at the masks on exhibit.

Venetian Glass and Art

Venetian glassmaking is well known around the world for its fine craftsmanship and aesthetic appeal. Venetian glassmaking has a more than a thousand-year history, and it is still a thriving industry today.

Here is a description of Venetian glass and art, along with information on how to learn more about this intriguing facet of Venetian culture:

- **Murano Island:** Known as the birthplace of Venetian glassmaking, Murano is a small island close to Venice. When you go to Murano, you can see how glass is made firsthand and tour the island's many glass studios, workshops, and galleries. You may watch expert glass blowers at work, learn about the complex methods they use, and even make direct purchases of one-of-a-kind glass creations from the craftspeople.

- **Glassblowing demos:** There are numerous glass studios in Venice that provide glass blowing demos, where talented artisans display their skill and produce stunning glass objects in front of your very eyes.

You can understand the challenging procedure of shaping and working with molten glass through these demonstrations, which also let you appreciate the talent and creativity required.

- **Glass Museums:** There are various glass museums in Venice where you may learn about the development of Venetian glass art. On Murano Island, the Murano Glass Museum (Museo del Vetro), which houses a sizable collection of both vintage and modern glass objects, is a must-see. In the centre of Venice, the Glass Museum in the Palazzo Giustinian houses a significant collection of Venetian glass artwork.

- Venice is home to a plethora of glass galleries and shops where you may peruse and buy magnificent glass works. These locations display the enormous talent and ingenuity of Venetian glass craftsmen through their elaborate sculptures, delicate glass jewellery, and decorative objects.

  You can enjoy the wide variety of Venetian glass art's styles and designs by perusing these galleries and stores.

- Jewellery and accessories made of glass: Venetian glass is frequently crafted into exquisite jewellery and accessories. Venetian glass jewellery is highly sought after because of its distinctive beauty, ranging from vibrant glass beads to elaborate necklaces, earrings, and bracelets. To find these wearable works of art, go to artisan fairs or specialised jewellery shops.

- **Glass Art Events and Festivals**: Venice hosts events and festivals all through the year that honour the craft of glassmaking. A famous occasion that features the best in modern glass art and design through exhibitions, workshops, and special events is the Glass Week in Murano.

These events offer chances to interact with glass artists, go to lectures and workshops, and see the most recent advancements in Venetian glass art.

By investigating Venetian glass and art, you can learn about the city's extensive artistic legacy and observe the extraordinary talent of glassmakers. You can buy a piece of Venetian glass artwork as a souvenir of your trip whether you visit Murano Island, tour glass museums, or peruse the galleries and shops in Venice.

Gondola Rides and Serenades

When visiting Venice, gondola rides and serenades are must-do activities. What you should know about these romantic and customary acts is as follows:

- **Gondola Rides:** Many tourists consider taking a gondola ride through Venice's scenic canals to be a must-do activity. Traditional Venetian rowing boats called gondolas are prized for their slender and refined appearance.

  You can take in Venice's gorgeous architecture, bridges, and winding passageways as you float around the tranquil waterways.

- **Gondoliers:** Skilled boatmen who operate gondolas are known as gondoliers. They dress in traditional striped shirts and are renowned for their skill in operating the boats and giving visitors an enjoyable experience. While guiding you along the canals, gondoliers frequently give amusing anecdotes and interesting facts about the city.

- **Serenades**: Serenades, frequently performed by musicians on board gondolas, give your voyage an additional air of romance and charm. Serenaders frequently perform traditional Italian music, such as love ballads or well-known tunes, to heighten the atmosphere of romance.
- M
An exceptional and entrancing environment is created by the tranquil music and the acoustic qualities of the canals.

- **Routes and Duration**: Depending on the route and package you select, gondola rides can last anywhere from 30 minutes to an hour. The Grand Canal and the more secluded, lesser canals in Venice are popular itineraries. You can choose a pre-planned itinerary or discuss your preferences with the gondolier.

- Gondola rides can be a bit pricey, particularly during the busiest travel seasons. Prices frequently vary depending on elements including the length of the trip, the route, and whether a serenade is included.

To avoid any misconceptions, it's critical to establish the price up front. To cut costs, you may also haggle over the price or think about taking a gondola with another passenger.

- **Gondola Rides at Sunset and at Night:** If you want a truly magical experience, think about going on a gondola ride at sunset or at night. The romantic mood created by the city's lit architecture or the warm glow of the setting sun can take the experience to new heights.

- Gondola rides can be booked on the spot at many gondola stations across Venice, but it's advised to reserve in advance to secure your desired time and guarantee a smooth experience. You can make reservations directly with gondoliers, via tour companies, or online.

- A gondola ride accompanied by a song is a romantic and wonderful way to discover Venice's gorgeous waterways. You can learn about the city's fascinating past, take in its natural beauty, and make lifelong impressions.

PRACTICAL TIPS FOR A SMOOTH TRIP

Here is some useful advice to bear in mind to have a smooth and pleasurable vacation to Venice:

- Making a Plan To make the most of your visit, do your research and organise your trip in advance. Think about the sights you want to see, the areas you want to check out, and any festivals or events you want to go to. To minimise disappointment, make reservations for lodging, popular activities, and restaurants.

- **Pack sensibly:** The weather in Venice may be erratic, so bring clothing that can be worn in a variety of settings. Since you'll be wandering around the city, you must have comfortable walking shoes. Never leave home without such necessities as sunscreen, a hat, and a reusable water bottle.

- **Stay Central**: To make it simpler to access important attractions and public transportation, pick lodging in or close to the city centre. You can enjoy Venice's convenience and charm while cutting down on travel time by staying strategically located.

- **Investigate Off-Peak Times:** Venice can be congested, particularly during the busiest travel seasons. To avoid crowds, think about visiting popular locations early in the morning or later in the evening. This makes it possible for you to have a more leisurely and engaging experience.

- Respect Local Customs: Become familiar with regional manners and customs. Respecting Venice's customs and traditions is crucial because the city has a rich cultural history. When visiting churches and other religious buildings, dress modestly and pay attention to noise levels, especially in neighbourhoods.

- Keep an eye on your possessions at all times because Venice is known for its busy rivers and congested streets. Use a lockable bag or backpack and avoid carrying big amounts of cash or valuables to stave off pickpockets.

- **Use Public Transportation**: Although Venice is a pedestrian-friendly city, you might want to use the Vaporetto (water bus) system to travel further distances or explore surrounding islands. Learn the routes and times, then purchase a travel pass that meets your needs.

- **Try the local cuisine:** There are many great regional foods available in Venice. Venetian specialties include cicchetti (little tapas-style appetisers), fresh seafood, risotto, and tiramisu should not be missed. To find local products and fresh produce, explore your local markets.

- Learn a Few Basic Italian Words: Although many Venetians understand English, learning a few simple Italian words will improve your interactions and demonstrate respect for the local way of life. Locals will appreciate simple salutations and kind language.

- **Enjoy the Ambiance**: Venice is a singular and alluring city, so take some time to take it all in. Explore the beautiful districts, meander through the little alleyways, and admire the canals' exquisite beauty. Accept the slower pace of life and experience Venice's enchanted atmosphere.

You may enjoy a smooth trip to Venice and immerse yourself in the city's rich history, culture, and beauty by paying attention to this useful advice.

Staying Safe in Venice

Although tourists are generally safe in Venice, it's always advisable to take security measures to protect your safety and well-being. Here are some recommendations to keep you safe when touring Venice:

- **Be Wary of Your Possessions:** Be particularly watchful of your possessions while you're in a busy environment or using public transit. Use a safe bag or backpack and store valuables like cash, electronics, and passports there.

- **Avoid Tourist Fraud**: Venice is a major tourist destination, therefore frauds and pickpocketing are a given. Be wary of people who approach you with unsolicited offers and be alert to common frauds like phoney petitions or diversionary tactics intended to take your possessions.

- **Utilise Reliable Transportation**: When travelling in Venice, only utilise authorised taxis, recognized water buses (vaporettos), and water taxis (motoscafi). Unlicensed individuals selling transportation services should be avoided since they could not be dependable or safe.

- **Avoid Empty or Isolated Streets**: When strolling through Venice, especially at night, stay in areas that are well-lit and populated. The big tourist locations are generally safe to wander around in, but be careful in the more residential areas.

- **Respect Local Customs and Laws:** To prevent any

unintentional infractions, familiarise oneself with local laws and customs. For instance, keep the volume down, dress modestly when visiting places of worship, and adhere to any rules or guidelines posted in museums and other attractions.

- Venice is a city of canals, therefore exercise caution when strolling close to the water's edge, especially if there are no barriers or guardrails present. Do not overhang bridges or take undue chances close to canals.

- Venice may get hot during the summer, so make sure to drink enough water to stay hydrated and protect yourself from the sun. For sun protection, put on sunscreen, a hat, and light, breathable clothing.

- **Use Reputable Services and Accommodations:** Reserve lodging, excursions, and other services from respectable suppliers. To confirm the validity and calibre of your reservations, read reviews, look for professional qualifications, and use reputable booking sites.

- Know the local emergency numbers, including the universal emergency number (112) that can be used everywhere in Europe and the local police number (113). Keep these phone numbers handy for rapid access in an emergency.

- Above all, trust your instincts and pay attention to your surroundings. Remove yourself from the situation if something or someone makes you feel uneasy and ask for help if necessary.

You may have a safe and pleasurable trip in Venice by being cautious, being aware of your surroundings, and paying attention to these safety recommendations. Always put your security first and take essential safety measures while you are there.

Etiquette and Customs

To demonstrate respect for the city's culture and traditions, visitors to Venice should be aware of the local etiquette and customs. Here are some etiquette pointers to remember:

- **Dress Respectfully:** When visiting churches and other religious buildings, wear modest clothing. Shorts, tank tops, and tiny skirts are examples of revealing apparel that both men and women ought to avoid wearing. In places of worship, you should cover your shoulders and knees and take your caps off.

- Italians typically shake hands and make direct eye contact when greeting one another. An appropriate "Buongiorno" (good morning) or "Buona sera" (good evening) goes a long way when conversing with locals or service personnel. It's polite to introduce yourself before striking up a discussion.

- **Punctuality**: Italians value being on time, so make an effort to get to appointments, tours, and dinner reservations on time. It ensures a smooth flow of events and demonstrates respect for other people's time.

- In restaurants, it's customary to wait for the host or waiter to seat you before ordering. Remember that some restaurants might have designated tables or specified seating configurations. Use forks and knives properly when you are dining, and keep your hands on the table but not your elbows. Wait until everyone at the table has been served before you begin to eat.

- Tipping is not required in Italy because a service charge is frequently added to the bill. For great service, it is appreciated if you leave a tiny extra tip. You can leave a tip in the amount of 5–10% of the total bill, or you can round up the bill.

- **Language**: Even though English is widely spoken in tourist regions, it's always nice to acquire a few fundamental Italian phrases and utilise them while speaking with locals. Respecting the local way of life can be demonstrated by using simple greetings like "Buongiorno" (good morning), "Grazie" (thank you), and "prego" (you're welcome).

- **Noise Levels**: Because Venice is a city with a lot of people living and working there, it's necessary to pay attention to noise levels, particularly in residential areas. When possible, keep conversations and disturbances quiet, especially in the early morning and late evening.

- **Photography**: When taking pictures, be aware of your surroundings. Don't hinder views or block routes. Pay heed to signage and follow any rules if photography is restricted or forbidden inside some cathedrals and museums.

- **Queuing**: Lines or queues are frequently seen in major tourist sites. Waiting your time and avoiding the front of the line shows respect for others. This holds for crowded areas such as public transportation, attractions, and other places.

- **Respect the City**: Venice is a special and delicate city, thus it's crucial to respect the surroundings and abide by any laws or ordinances that may be in existence. Avoid leaving trash behind, causing damage to buildings or historic places, or acting in any way that could compromise the sensitive environment of the city.

Following these etiquette guidelines will help you respect Venice's traditions and make the most of your cultural visit. Remember that having respectful encounters with locals and other travellers can be facilitated by showing little regard and understanding.

Language and Communication

Italian is the primary language used in Venice for communication. It is usually appreciated when travellers make an effort to acquire a few basic Italian words, even if English is widely spoken in many tourist locations, especially in hotels, restaurants, and shops. What you need to know about language and communication in Venice is as follows:

- **Italian:** The official tongue of Venice and the rest of Italy is Italian. Knowing a few basic Italian phrases will help you get around the city and communicate with the locals because they speak it in their daily lives.

- Learning some fundamental Italian phrases will tremendously improve your time in Venice. A few helpful greetings to learn include "Buongiorno" (good morning), "Buona sera" (good evening), "Grazie" (thank you), "prego" (you're welcome), "mi scusi" (pardon me), and "Parla inglese?" (do you speak English?).

- **English Proficiency:** Venetians who work in the tourism sector speak English well in several popular tourist sites. English proficiency is frequently found among tour guides, restaurant servers, and hotel workers. Even so, it's still considerate to start your greetings in Italian before switching to English.

- **Non-Verbal Communication:** In Venice, non-verbal communication is also important. Paying attention to these indicators will help you understand discussions and interactions because Italians frequently use hand gestures and facial expressions to convey meaning.

- **Phrasebook or Translation applications:** To help you with basic conversation when necessary, think about bringing a phrasebook or using translation applications on your smartphone. When communicating with locals who might have low English skills, these techniques might be extremely useful.

- **Respect and Courtesy**: When interacting with natives, it's crucial to be courteous and respectful. Positive encounters can be greatly improved by using simple courtesy expressions like "per favour" (please) and "scuba" (pardon me).

- **Solutions for Language Barriers:** When communicating in circumstances where there may be a language barrier, try using plain English, speaking slowly, or utilising gestures. Locals are frequently sympathetic and eager to help you in any way they can.

- **Cultural Exchange:** Take advantage of the chance to converse with locals and learn about their way of life. A smile and a warm demeanour can establish connections even if your language abilities are weak and enhance your time in Venice.

Remember that even if you don't speak Italian well, the people there will still appreciate your attempt to interact with them. When you need assistance or an explanation, don't be afraid to ask because most Venetians are pleasant and happy to help you in English or with simple gestures.

Essential Packing List

It's crucial to pack for your vacation to Venice by taking the season, weather, and activities you'll be doing into account. Here is a list of things you must pack to assist you get ready for your visit:

Clothing:

- Pack supportive and comfy shoes for strolling over cobblestone streets because Venice is best explored on foot.

- Lightweight clothing that breathes: Pack seasonal attire that is suitable for the weather. In the summer, use lightweight, breathable fabrics. Pack a light jacket and layers for the cooler months.

- Dress modestly when attending churches: Pack modest clothes that cover your shoulders and knees if you intend to visit churches or other religious locations.

- **Swimwear**: Bring swimwear if you're travelling during the summer or if you intend to visit the beaches.

Weather Defence:

- Pack a small umbrella or a lightweight raincoat because Venice can occasionally suffer sprinkles of rain.

- Pack sunscreen and a wide-brimmed hat for sun protection because the summer heat can be very strong.

Travel necessities:
- A valid passport and any other relevant travel documents: Make sure you have a current passport as well as any necessary visas or travel authorizations well before your journey.

- Carry enough cash in the local currency (Euros) for little purchases, and have a credit/debit card on hand for bigger ones. In Venice, ATMs are widely available.

- Bring a travel adaptor if your plugs are different since Venice uses Type C and Type L electrical outlets.

- Portable charger: Use a portable charger to keep your electronic devices charged while you're on the go.

- Carry a travel guidebook or have maps on hand to help you traverse Venice and make plans for your day.

- Copies of significant paperwork: Make copies of your passport, travel insurance, and other crucial papers, and store them somewhere apart from where the originals are kept.

Personal Effects

- Personal hygiene items: Bring your toothbrush, toothpaste, shampoo, conditioner, and any other necessary items.

- **Medication:** If you need to take prescription medication, make sure you have enough for the entire trip.

- Carry a first aid package that includes bandages, painkillers, and any other required medicines or supplies.

- Towel for travel: When travelling, it can be helpful to have a small, quick-drying towel, especially if you intend to visit beaches or participate in water sports.

Accessories and electronics:

- Mobile phone and charger: Always keep a charger or portable power bank on hand for your phone to stay charged.

- Camera: Use a quality camera or smartphone to capture the stunning sights of Venice.

- Bring the appropriate adapters and chargers for your electrical gadgets.

Miscellaneous:

- Have a modest day backpack or tote bag on hand to carry your necessities while touring the city.

- Carrying a reusable water bottle can help you stay hydrated because Venice's tap water is safe to drink.

- Travel locks: Use travel locks on your bags to protect your things.

- Consider buying travel insurance to safeguard yourself from unanticipated circumstances like trip cancellations or medical emergencies.

- To avoid any problems at the airport, don't forget to check your airline's luggage policies and weight restrictions before you pack. Leaving some extra room in your suitcase for any souvenirs or other items you might buy while on your trip is also a smart idea.

Useful Phrases

Knowing a few basic Italian words will tremendously improve your trip to Venice and facilitate interaction with the people. The following keywords should be added to your vocabulary:

Greetings and Foundational Words:
- Ciao! (Hello!/Hi!)
- Buongiorno! (Good morning!/Good day!)
- Buonasera! (Good evening!)
- Buonanotte! (Good night!)
- Grazie! (Thank you!)
- Prego! (You're welcome!)
- Mi scusi! (Excuse me!)
- Per favore! (Please!)
- Non capisco. (I don't understand.)
- Parla inglese? (Do you speak English?)

Introductions and Polite Phrases:

- Mi chiamo [your name]. (My name is [your name].)
- Piacere di conoscerti. (Nice to meet you.)
- Come star? (How are you?)
- Molto bene, grazie. (Very well, thank you.)
- Mi dispiace. (I'm sorry.)
- Scusi, dov'è [place or landmark]? (Excuse me, where is [place or landmark]?)
- Posso avere il conto, per favore? (Can I have the bill, please?)

Ordering Food and Drinks:

- Vorrei un caffè, per favore. (I would like a coffee, please.)
- Vorrei una birra/acqua/vino, per favore. (I would like a beer/water/wine, please.)
- Vorrei il menù, per favore. (I would like the menu, please.)

- Cosa consiglia? (What do you recommend?)
- Vorrei ordinare [dish or item], per favore. (I would like to order [dishes or items], please.)
- Il conto, per favore. (The bill, please.)

Asking for Directions:

- Scusi, dov'è la stazione? (Excuse me, where is the train station?)
- Scusi, come si arriva a [place or landmark]? (Excuse me, how do I get to [place or landmark]?)
- È lontano? (Is it far?)
- A destra. (To the right.)
- A sinistra. (To the left.)
- Dritto. (Straight ahead.)
- Grazie mille! (Thank you very much!)

Emergency Phrases:

- Aiuto! (Help!)

- Chiamate un'ambulanza! (Call an ambulance!)
- Ho bisogno di un dottore. (I need a doctor.)
- Sono perso/a. (I am lost.)
- Ho perso il mio portafoglio. (I lost my wallet.)

Always speak slowly and clearly, and if necessary, don't be afraid to make gestures or point at things. Locals are appreciative of your efforts and frequently willing to help you.

In addition to improving your relationships in Venice and demonstrating respect for the local language and culture, learning a few basic words can go a long way.

Useful Resources

There are several helpful tools you may use to organise your trip to Venice, collect knowledge, and facilitate your travels. Here are some sources we advise using:

Licensed travel websites:

- Venezia Unica. it, the Venice Tourism Board's official website, offers comprehensive information about destinations, activities, and travel considerations.

- Comune.venezia.it, the City of Venice's official website, provides details on neighbourhood services, current events, and news.

Online travel communities and forums:
- On TripAdvisor (tripadvisor.com), you can ask questions and find

answers from other visitors who have been to Venice. TripAdvisor offers a huge collection of reviews, suggestions, and forums.

- The r/Venice subreddit on Reddit is a forum where you can interact with other tourists, locals, and expats to get advice and swap stories.

Mobile applications

- You may use Google Maps or Apple Maps to find your way around Venice and get driving, public transportation, and walking directions.

- The official app of the Venice Tourism Board provides offline maps, audio guides, and details on sights, events, and transit.

- Using TripIt or TripCase, you can keep track of your travel plans, flight information, and hotel reservations all in one location.

Local knowledge:

- You can get maps, brochures, and individualised recommendations for your trip from local tourist information centres like the Venice Tourist Information Office or the Venice Tourism Board's Visitor Centers.

- Talking to residents or hotel staff can also yield insightful information and suggestions for off-the-beaten-path activities in Venice.

Online travel articles and travel blogs:
- Numerous travel blogs and websites provide first-person tales,

advice, and suggestions for visiting Venice. There are numerous posts on Venice on well-known travel blogs like "The Blonde Abroad," "Wandering Earl," and "Nomadic Matt" that might inspire and offer useful tips.

- Keep in mind to cross-reference data from several sources to guarantee its accuracy and relevance. This will enable you to make well-informed choices and customise your trip itinerary to suit your needs.

Website and Apps for Venice travel

There are several helpful websites and apps you can use to plan your trip to Venice that can offer useful information, help with navigation, and improve your entire travel experience. The following are some suggested websites and apps for travelling to Venice:

Websites:

- The official website of the Venice Tourism Board, Venezia Unica (Venezia Unica. it), provides complete details on Venice's attractions, events, transit, and services. Additionally, it offers a platform for purchasing tickets for numerous services and activities.

- The official website of the City of Venice, Comune di Venezia (comune.venezia.it), offers details about neighbourhood services, news, events, and laws. It can help gain access to necessary resources and comprehend how the city is run.

- TripAdvisor (tripadvisor.com): TripAdvisor provides reviews, suggestions, and forums where you can learn from other travellers, locate top-rated eateries, hotels, and attractions, and assess lodging costs.

- You may navigate Venice using Google Maps (maps.google.com) or Apple Maps (maps.apple.com), which also provide driving, walking, and public transportation instructions and real-time traffic updates.

- The website of the regional public transportation provider ACTV (active.avmspa.it) offers details about vaporetto (water bus) schedules, routes, and prices. Additionally, it provides online ticket purchasing choices.

Apps:

- App for iOS and Android that offers offline maps, audio guides, and details on Venice's sights, events, and transit is the official travel guide for the city. While offline, it can be a useful tool for getting around the city.

- To conveniently tour Venice, use Google Maps (iOS, Android) or Apple Maps (iOS). These well-known navigation apps provide real-time directions, transit information, and practical features like street view and reviews.

- The official ACTV app for iOS and Android gives you access to

Vaporetto timetables, routes, and ticket alternatives. Additionally, it offers notifications and real-time updates for service modifications.

- You may get reviews, ratings, and suggestions for restaurants, hotels, sights, and activities in Venice using the TripAdvisor app (iOS, Android). It can aid in decision-making and the discovery of hidden treasures.

- The Rick Steves app, Rick Steves Audio Europe (iOS, Android), provides free audio tours with detailed commentary on well-known Venice attractions. You may discover the history and culture of the city while going at your own leisure.

To get the most of these tools, be sure to download and install any essential apps before your travel and have access to stable internet connectivity. Additionally, integrating online sources with travel manuals and insider tips can offer a complete and all-encompassing vacation experience in Venice.

Emergency Contacts

It's crucial to have access to emergency contacts when visiting Venice in case of any unforeseen circumstances or emergencies. Here are some crucial Venice emergency phone numbers:

Services for Emergencies:

- Police/Fire/Ambulance in Case of Emergency: 112 (This is the emergency number for Europe that is functional in all EU members, including Italy.)

- Carabinieri: 112 or 113 (military police of Italy)

- 113 State Police (Polizia di Stato)

- Number of firefighters (Vigili del Fuoco): 115

- Emergency Care: 118

Tourist Control:

- Consulates and Embassies: Polizia di Stato - Ufficio di Polizia per il Turismo (Tourist Police): +39 041 529 8711.

- U.S. Embassy in Italy (24-hour assistance): +39 06 46741

  To reach the British Embassy in Italy, dial +39 06 4220 0001.

- For assistance, call the Canadian Embassy in Italy at +39 06 854 44 291.

- (24-hour assistance) Australian Embassy in Italy: +39 06 8527 21

- Consulate or embassy of your particular nation: Before your travel, make a note of the contact information.

Medical Centers and Hospitals:

- Ospedale dell'Angelo (Mestre): +39 041 260 1111 Ospedale SS. Giovanni e Paolo: +39 041 529 4111

- It's also a good idea to keep your lodging's location and phone number nearby in case you need them in an emergency or to request assistance.

Always put your safety and well-being first in an emergency, and don't be afraid to ask for assistance from the proper emergency services.

CONCLUSION

As we come to a close with this Venice travel guide, we sincerely hope that it has given you useful details, advice, and insights to make the most of your time there. Venice provides a genuinely immersive travel experience with its rich history, beautiful architecture, and distinctive charm.

Venetian attractions and undiscovered gems abound, from touring the famous St. Mark's Square and Basilica to ambling around the charming neighbourhoods of Cannaregio, Dorsoduro, and beyond.

Every traveller may find something to enthral them in Venice, whether they are interested in the city's rich cultural history, experiencing authentic Venetian food, or just taking a gondola ride around the canals.

Consider things like the ideal time to visit, how long you should stay, and your budget when planning your vacation. Use the Vaporetto system and other available transit choices to efficiently move around the city. Don't forget to immerse yourself in the regional customs, festivals, and culture that make Venice so special.

Prioritise your safety, observe the regional customs and etiquette, and carry the essential travel documentation as you go out on your Venice excursion. Learn who to call in case of emergency, and keep their numbers handy.

Last but not least, Venice is a place of enduring beauty and appeal. It's a location where romance, art, and history all converge to produce a genuinely magical experience. So get started on your trip to Venice, explore its canals and bridges, and make lifelong memories.

Bon voyage! (Enjoy your journey!)

Final Thoughts and Recommendations

Here are some closing thoughts and suggestions to help you make the most of your trip as we draw to a close with this travel guide to Venice:

- **Embrace Venice's distinctiveness:** With its intricate canal network, beautiful architecture, and extensive cultural history, Venice is unlike any other city in the world. Spend some time admiring it and becoming lost in its alluring aura.

- **Get lost in the backstreets**: While the big sites are interesting, don't be hesitant to stray from the crowds and discover Venice's more sedate areas and secret nooks. You never know what wonderful discoveries you might make.

- Venice can get congested throughout the day, especially in popular spots, so take advantage of the early mornings and late evenings. Take advantage of the slower times in the mornings and evenings when you may appreciate the beauty of the city without as many people around.

- **Try some local cuisine**: Indulge in some of the tasty treats that Venice has to offer. Try classic delicacies like risotto al nero di sepia (squid ink risotto) and sarde in saor (sweet and sour sardines). Don't forget to drink some local Venetian wine with your dinner.

- Be prepared for long lines at major locations like the Doge's Palace and St. Mark's Basilica. To save time and make the most of your visit, think about purchasing tickets in advance or choosing skip-the-line options.

- Aside from the city, there are many places to see and things to do: For a fresh perspective on the area, consider taking day trips to the adjacent islands of Murano, Burano, and Torcello or going to the quaint Venetian villas on the mainland.

- Venice is a photographer's delight; capture the splendour there. Bring your camera so you may record the mesmerising views, exquisite details, and unguarded moments that make Venice so alluring.

- Be respectful of the city and its inhabitants; Venice is a bustling neighbourhood. Recognize how tourism affects the environment and take care when you go. Be respectful of the city's regulations, save energy and water, and show consideration for the neighbourhood.

- Venice is designed to be experienced at a leisurely pace, so take your time and enjoy it. Spend some time sitting at a café, watching the gondolas go by, and taking in the distinctive atmosphere of the city.

- Keep an open mind and be willing to accept the unexpected because Venice will never fail to amaze you. Accept the chance encounters, have an open mind to new things, and watch as Venice's enchantment plays out in front of you.

We hope that these suggestions will enable you to get the most out of your trip to Venice. I hope your time in this fascinating city is full of treasured memories and life-changing events. Bon voyage!

Fond Farewell to Venice

Let the memories of Venice's picturesque canals, alluring architecture, and rich history stay in your heart as you say goodbye to this magical city. We hope that your time in Venice has been nothing less than amazing because Venice has a way of leaving its guests with a lasting memory.

Remember the spectacular beauty of St. Mark's Square and Basilica, the splendour of the Doge's Palace, the vivid colours of Burano, the fine craftsmanship of Murano, and the serenity of Torcello as you think back on your tour. These encounters have created a tapestry of priceless memories that you will carry with you for a very long time.

Take the awe, admiration for art and culture, and capacity to slow down and appreciate the beauty of ordinary moments with you as you depart from Venice. Allow the echoes of gondoliers' singing and the sound of water lapping to serve as a reminder of Venice's distinct charm.

Even though you are leaving this magnificent city, Venice will always have a particular place in your heart. Keep its spirit close to you as you move on, and may it motivate you to see more of the globe with a spirit of adventure and curiosity.

We appreciate you allowing this travel guide to be a part of your journey. We wish you safe travels and forward to seeing you again in Venice.

Welcome back, Venice!